Ne

O

Dr SIEGLINDE McGEE

Set in 10.5 pt Garamond

ISBN 9781794555013

Cover photo by Sieglinde McGee

Disclaimer

ABOUT THE AUTHOR

Sieglinde discovered horse racing by chance on Grand National day 1982 and was instantly hooked, reading and watching everything she could about it. She started writing on the subject in the summer of 1983, began keeping personal databases on racing and pedigrees the following year, and got her first job in racing five years after that – doing course wires (tipping) and bloodstock sales reports for *The Sporting Life*, maintaining a small pedigree database, and producing press releases for a major stud.

She has been widely published on racing and pedigrees over the past three decades, wrote and produced her own non-published 'Timeform Annual-style' books for several years in the 1990s, has been writing for *The Irish Field* since the spring of 2000, and on her own website (www.sieglindemcgee.com) for the past two and a half years.

In 2005, she was conferred with a doctorate from Trinity College Dublin for a thesis titled *Behavioural Reactivity and Ensuing Temperamental Traits in Young Thoroughbred Racehorses (Equus caballus)* – the culmination of four years of postgraduate research. She is also a graduate of Dublin City University and of the world-famous Thoroughbred Breeding course at the Irish National Stud, and she taught in Trinity College Dublin and for Oscail (now DCU Connected) for several years.

ALSO BY THE AUTHOR

Racing / pedigrees:
European Group 1 Winners of 2018. Independently published, 2018. 396 pages. Paperback & ebook

Other:
Key Research & Study Skills in Psychology. SAGE, London, 2010. 210 pages. Hardback, paperback & ebook

CONTENTS

** New to the northern hemisphere but is a proven Group 1 sire in Australia from his first two crops.

INTRODUCTION

One of the fascinating aspects of the thoroughbred breeding season is to see how the new recruits settle in and how they are supported. Another is to see the first foals by the previous year's newcomers. In 2019, there are more than 40 new stallions for breeders to consider, 10 in Ireland, 18 in the UK, and 14 in France. They include classic heroes, sprinters, milers, middle-distances horses, a champion stayer, two-year-old stars, an established Australian Group 1 sire making the journey north for the first time, and even one of last year's top young hurdlers.

The race record and pedigree of each are reviewed, along with comments on their future prospects. There is also a series of indexes in which they are organised: by stud, sire, grandsire, great-grandsire, broodmare sire, date of their earliest win, the highest grade in which they won, the distances over which they won group races, the ages at which they achieved those feats, the going on which they got those wins, and by their fee.

Where the are other stallions by the sire of the horse being reviewed, a selection of these is listed in his summary details section. The (Gr1) or similar notation shown by their name represents the highest level at which they have, so far, had at least one winner. If their eldest offspring are two-year-olds, yearlings or foals, then that is indicated instead.

Readers may notice that some horses have not been given a suffix with their names, in pedigree charts or the various indexes. This is not an error or omission. The suffix indicates the country in which the horse was born, but those who were born in Ireland or in Great Britain did not get suffixes until 1988. Therefore, horses born in those countries before that year do not have one.

Best of luck to all of the studs and breeders, in 2019 and beyond!

Sieglinde McGee
10 January 2019

IRELAND

NEW SIRES OF 2019

GUSTAV KLIMT (IRE)

Two of the things that we look for when assessing the future stallion potential of any new recruit are the effectiveness of his male line and the presence or absence of successful stallions in the distaff side of his pedigree. Scoring well on these measures are by no means a guarantee that he will excel in his new role, but his odds of becoming a sire of at least one or two Group 1 winners shorten if he is suitably well bred for the role. There are, of course, many good horses whose sire was of little note, one-hit wonders or even one among a handful of talented horses he fathered in an otherwise unremarkable career. There are also plenty of horses who are bred to make their mark on the track, but not necessarily at stud, and too many who promise much and appear well qualified, only to disappoint.

Gustav Klimt, however, appears to have everything going for him. He was a talented juvenile, a classic-placed stakes winner at three, and he has an outstanding stallion's pedigree. Not only is he by one of the greatest sires of all time – a horse who has a double-digit tally of sons with at least one top-level winner to their name at stud – but he is out of a stakes-winning closer-than-half-sister to a Group 1 scorer and leading international sire. Indeed, his dam is also a full-sister to another stallion of note.

This makes him a likely source of stakes and pattern winners, and a shade of odds-on to sire at least one who can hit the target at Group 1 level. The quality of the mares that he receives will, of course, be important, as will the physical characteristics that his offspring inherit, but it is fair to say that Gustav Klimt could prove himself to be one of the best-value new recruits of 2019.

He was trained by Aidan O'Brien, finished unplaced on his debut over six furlongs at the Curragh, but won a maiden over seven at that venue in early July. He was an odds-on favourite for the Group 2 Superlative Stakes at Newmarket barely a fortnight later, and despite encountering trouble in running, he created a favourable impression in getting up to win by a head from Nebo. He was not seen out again that year but went into winter quarters with a 112p rating from Timeform.

It was surprising that his seven-furlong listed success at Leopardstown in mid-April 2018 was his final win because he went on to perform with merit in a string of Group 1 contests, finishing the campaign on a Timeform mark of 123. He was out of the frame behind stablemate Saxon Warrior in the 2000 Guineas at Newmarket, finished third to Romanised in the Irish 2000 Guineas at the Curragh, failed by just half a length to beat Without Parole in the St James's Palace Stakes at Ascot, and then took third in the Group 1 Prix Jean Prat at Deauville, which was won by Intellogent. His penultimate attempt at a mile saw him finish a two-length fourth to Lightning Spear in the Sussex Stakes at Goodwood, he was only beaten by a total of a length and a half when fourth to One Master in the seven-furlong Prix de la Foret at ParisLongchamp in October, and with heavy ground adding an element of a stamina test to the six-furlong Sprint Cup at Haydock the month before, he finished an honourable third, beaten just a half-length and a neck by The Tin Man and Brando.

That latter performance placed him high among the speediest representatives of his great sire, Galileo (by Sadler's Wells), and it was not a surprise that he could produce such a run given the distaff side of his family. His dam, Massara (by Danehill), was a listed sprint winner who finished runner-up in the Group 2 Prix Robert Papin, his siblings include juvenile listed sprint winner Cuff (by Galileo), and his 'uncles' include Invincible Spirit (by Green Desert) and Kodiac (by Danehill).

Massarra is, of course, a full-sister to the latter, and the Tally-Ho Stud stallion had an outstanding season in 2018, on the track and in the auction ring, and spearheaded by the Group 1 victories of Best Solution and Fairyland. Invincible Spirit, on the other hand, is the flag bearer at the Irish National Stud, and his long list of Group 1 stars includes Eqtidaar, Magna Grecia, and Royal Meeting, each of whom won at the highest level in 2018. The pedigrees and racing records of each of that quintet are reviewed in *European Group 1 Winners of 2018*.

There may be an impression that these family connections made Gustav Klimt all but guaranteed to become one of his sire's milers rather than middle-distance horses, but he could have gone either way. His siblings include the mile juvenile Italian Group 1 scorer Nayarra (by Cape Cross), but two of his half-sisters have produced stakes winners at almost 12 furlongs – one of whom picked up a third-place finish in the Group 2 Ribblesdale Stakes – his dam is also a half-sister to the middle-distance pattern winners Sadian (by Shirley Heights) and Acts Of Grace (by Bahri), and his grandam is the Group 1 Prix de Diane (French Oaks) heroine Rafha (by Kris).

That classic star is a half-sister to Group 3 Blandford Stakes winner Chiang Mai (by Sadler's Wells) – the dam of Group 1 Pretty Polly Stakes scorer Chinese White (by Dalakhani) – and to four others who deserve mention due to the exploits of their descendants rather than anything they achieved themselves.

Al Anood (by Danehill) was placed in a listed race but is notable as the dam of South African champion stayer and Group 2 winner Enaad (by High Chaparral) and of Pride Of Dubai (by Street Cry), the dual Australian juvenile Group 1 scorer who is a reserve-shuttle member of the Coolmore stallion team. His first European foals made up to 82,000gns at auction in 2018.

Rafha's stakes-placed half-sister Fayfa (by Slip Anchor) is the third dam of Group 2 winner and Group 1 New Zealand Oaks runner-up Contessa Vanessa (by Bullbars), and her full-sister El Jazirah is the grandam of Group 3 scorer Master Carpenter (by Mastercraftsman), who is featured in the next section of this book. The other sibling of note is Wosaita (by Generous), and in addition to being the dam of Italian Group 3 winner Whazzis (by Desert Prince) and of Listed Chesham Stakes scorer Whazzat (by Daylami), she is the grandam of Grade 1 Matriarch Stakes heroine Uni (by More Than Ready) and also of the notably quick James Garfield (by Exceed And Excel), another new Irish stallion in 2019.

If you go back another generation then you will find that Eljazzi (by Artaius), the third dam of Gustav Klimt, was a half-sister to Group 2 Blandford Stakes winner Valley Forge, to classic-placed triple Group 3 scorer and subsequent champion sire Pitcairn, and to Dingle Bay, the winning dam of Group 1 Prix du Cadran star and successful National Hunt stallion Assessor (by Niniski). Each of that trio was by the classic-placed Sussex Stakes ace Petingo (by Petition). Pitcairn's offspring featured the Group 1 standouts Cairn Rouge and Ela-Mana-Mou, the former later an influential broodmare and the latter a classic sire.

Pedigree credentials like these, combined with his smart record at two and high-class one at three, suggest that Gustav Klimt could achieve anything at stud. He clearly got the 'speed gene' from his dam to go with the stamina one that Galileo passes on, and this gives him the potential to get everything from speedy juveniles up to middle-distance classic horses, and possibly even a Cup horse or two, from the right mare. Being able to sire good horses over a wide range of distances boosts a stallion's prospects of taking high rank, and all of the above makes this young horse one of the most intriguing additions to the stallion ranks this year.

SUMMARY DETAILS

Standing: Castlehyde Stud, Co Cork
Fee: €7,500
Career highlights: 3 wins inc bet365 Superlative Stakes (Gr2), Ballylinch 2000 Guineas Trial Stakes (L), 2nd St James's Palace Stakes (Gr1), 3rd Tattersalls Irish 2000 Guineas (Gr1), Prix Jean Prat (Gr1), 32Red Sprint Cup Stakes (Gr1)
Other stallions by his sire include: Cima De Triomphe (Gr1), Frankel (Gr1), Heliostatic (Gr1), Intello (Gr1), Nathaniel (Gr1), New Approach (Gr1), Rip Van Winkle (Gr1), Roderic O'Connor (Gr1), Ruler Of The World (Gr1), Sixties Icon (Gr1), Soldier Of Fortune (Gr1), Teofilo (Gr1), Treasure Beach (Gr1)

GUSTAV KLIMT (IRE) – bay 2015

Galileo (IRE)	Sadler's Wells (USA)	Northern Dancer (CAN)
		Fairy Bridge (USA)
	Urban Sea (USA)	Miswaki (USA)
		Allegretta
Massarra (GB)	Danehill (USA)	Danzig (USA)
		Razyana (USA)
	Rafha	Kris
		Eljazzi

JAMES GARFIELD (IRE)

Leading international sire Exceed And Excel (by Danehill) is one of the best of the reverse shuttle stallions and Darley's Kildangan Stud team member has a promising stallion prospect in James Garfield, the George Scott-trained colt who won the recent Group 2 Dubai Duty Free Mill Reef Stakes at as a juvenile and went close to scoring at the highest level at three.

He took that six-furlong contest by three-parts of a length from Invincible Army, with Nebo another half-length back in third, and this trio finished three and a half lengths clear of the fourth. It was his second win from six starts, he was still a maiden when taking third of 22 in the Listed Windsor Castle Stakes at Royal Ascot in June – which was won by Sound And Silence – he was not disgraced when fourth to Expert Eye in the Group 2 Qatar Vintage Stakes at Goodwood, and then failed by the narrowest of margins to beat Wells Farhh Go in the Group 3 Tattersalls Acomb Stakes at York. The latter two events are over seven furlongs. He then tried a mile at Del Mar on his final outing of the year but finished unplaced behind Mendelssohn in the Grade 1 Breeders' Cup Juvenile Turf.

That good juvenile record, which saw him rated 111 by Timeform, all but guaranteed that he would land a good berth at stud, but not just because of the current fashion for early two-year-old speed. James Garfield represents the powerful Danehill (by Danzig) sire line – albeit one that has had mixed early results – and he comes from the immediate family of two leading European sires, one of them responsible for a double-digit tally of Group 1-winning offspring.

His first start at three was in the Group 3 Al Basti World Greatwood Greenham Stakes over seven furlongs at Newbury, and it was a good one. He beat Expert Eye by three-quarters of a length, and although that rival improved considerably and starts his stallion career in 2019 as a Grade 1 star, James Garfield failed to win again in six subsequent tries. Indeed, his only time to make the frame was when finishing a half-length runner-up to Polydream in the Group 1 LARC Prix Maurice de Gheest over six and a half furlongs at Deauville in early August. This was the run that enabled him to complete the year on a Timeform rating of 124. His fourth-place (does not count for blacktype) to Sands Of Mali in the Group 2 Armstrong Aggregates Sandy Lane Stakes over six furlongs at Haydock in late May was another good effort.

Bred by owner Bill Gredley's Stetchworth & Middle Park Studs, James Garfield is the best of several winners out of Listed Chesham Stakes scorer Whazzat (by Daylami). Those include the stakes-placed miler The Shrew (by Dansili), but his dam's siblings include Unaided (by Dansili), an unplaced filly who has a notable daughter in the USA. That Chad Brown-trainee, Uni (by More Than Ready), was a nine-furlong listed scorer in France before crossing the Atlantic. She was third to New Money Honey in the Grade 1 Belmont Oaks Invitational Stakes over 10 furlongs, then runner-up in the Grade 2 Lake Placid Stakes over nine at Saratoga before, just a week before her young relation's Newbury success, she landed the Grade 2 Sands Point Stakes by a neck back at Belmont, again over nine furlongs. She was then fourth in the Grade 1 Queen Elizabeth II Challenge Cup over the same trip at Keeneland, returned to action as a four-year-old, and reeled off a four-timer that included three more blacktype events and culminated in a half-length of Daddy Is A Legend in the Grade 1 Matriarch Stakes over a mile at Del Mar in early December.

Whazzat is also a half-sister to the Italian Group 3 scorer Whazzis (by Desert Prince), but her dam, Wosaita (by Generous), is a daughter of Eljazzi (by Artaius) and that makes James Garfield another talented relation of a famous and stallion-producing family. Eljazzi is the dam of the Group 1 Prix de Diane (French Oaks) heroine Rafha (by Kris) and so is the grandam of Group 1 star Invincible Spirit (by Green Desert), of his blacktype-placed half-brother Kodiac (by Danehill), and of Group 2-placed stakes winner and notable broodmare Massarra (by Danehill). The first-named pair are important European sires, they had five European Group 1 winners between them in 2018, and Invincible Spirit already has several successful stallion sons to his name.

Massarra, on the other hand, is the dam of Group 1 Gran Criterium winner Nayarra (by Cape Cross), of additional juvenile blacktype scorers Cuff (by Galileo) and Wonderfully (by Galileo), and of that pair's full-brother Gustav Klimt who won the Group 2 bet365 Superlative Stakes at Newmarket as a juvenile before going on to become a classic-placed stakes winner at three. He too is a new sire in 2019. Eljazzi is also responsible for Chiang Mai (by Sadler's Wells), the Group 2 Blandford Stakes-winning dam of Group 1 Pretty Polly Stakes star Chinese White (by Dalakhani), and for Al Anood (by Danehill), the Australian-born dam of juvenile Group 1 star and young Coolmore reverse shuttle stallion Pride Of Dubai (by Street Cry) whose first foals made up to 82,000gns in 2018.

It is no surprise that Eljazzi proved to be such a good broodmare as this daughter of Yorkshire Oaks runner-up Border Bounty (by Bounteous) was a half-sister to the Petingo-sired (by Petition) trio of Group 1-placed Group 2 Blandford Stakes winner Valley Forge, classic-placed pattern scorer and leading sire Pitcairn, and Dingle Bay, the mare who gave us the Group 1-winning stayer and successful National Hunt sire Assessor (by Niniski). Pitcairn's standout pair were the Group 1 stars Cairn Rouge and Ela-Mana-Mou, the former an influential broodmare and the latter a classic sire.

James Garfield looks sure to prove popular in his new role and being a talented Danehill-line horse from the immediate family of Invincible Spirit and Kodiac there is every reason to hope that he can become a successful blacktype sire. His best representatives are likely to be effective in the five to 10-furlong range.

SUMMARY DETAILS

Standing: Rathbarry Stud, Co Cork
Fee: €7,000
Career highlights: 3 wins inc Dubai Duty Free Mill Reef Stakes (Gr2), Al Basti World Greatwood Greenham Stakes

(Gr3), 2nd LARC - Prix Maurice de Gheest (Gr1), Tattersalls
Acomb Stakes (Gr3), 3rd Windsor Castle Stakes (L)
Other stallions by his sire include: Excelebration (Gr1),
Helmet (Gr1), Bungle Inthejungle (Gr3), Exceedingly Good
(Gr3), Burwaaz (winners), Kuroshio (winners), Fulbright (2yo
of 2019), Outstrip (2yo), Sidestep (2yo), Buratino (yearlings),
Cotai Glory (foals)

JAMES GARFIELD (IRE) – bay 2015

Exceed And Excel (AUS)	Danehill (USA)	Danzig (USA)
		Razyana (USA)
	Patrona (USA)	Lomond (USA)
		Gladiolus (USA)
Whazzat (GB)	Daylami (IRE)	Doyoun
		Daltawa (IRE)
	Wosaita (GB)	Generous (IRE)
		Eljazzi

JUNGLE CAT (IRE)

When you have a horse who has been placed in as many stakes and pattern events as Jungle Cat has it comes as something of a surprise that his first win at that level arrives so late in his career. Godolphin's homebred six-year-old began his career in the Mark Johnston stable, winning a six-furlong Goodwood maiden and being placed in each of the Group 2 Coventry Stakes, Group 2 July Stakes, Group 2 Richmond Stakes and Group 2 Gimcrack Stakes – beaten just a nose by the following year's sprint champion Muhaarar in the latter!

At three, and now with Charlie Appleby, he chased home Adaay in the Listed Carnarvon Stakes at Newbury from just three starts, and he had been off the track for seven months when easily taking a six-furlong handicap at Meydan on his first start at four. He was then beaten by a nose in a Group 3 contest at the same venue, was fourth in the Group 1 Al Quoz Sprint, runner-up to Profitable in the Group 3 Palace House Stakes at Newmarket and then fourth behind that same horse in the Group 1 King's Stand Stakes at Ascot.

In 2017, he won a conditions race over seven furlongs at Haydock and was multiple blacktype-placed, and when he took the Group 2 Al Fahidi Fort over that same trip at Meydan at the start of the February 2018, it was his first outing since August. He beat Janoobi by three-parts of a length there and followed that with a two-and-a-quarter-length defeat of Timeform 127-rated star Ertijaal in a six-furlong conditions race at the same venue. It was no surprise, therefore, that Jungle Cat notched up his first Group 1 win shortly afterwards.

He beat now dual Grade 1 Breeders' Cup Turf Sprint star Stormy Liberal by half a length in the Group 1 Al Quoz Sprint over six furlongs, also at Meydan, and with that one's stablemate Conquest Tsunami another length and a half back in third and Irish raider Washington DC fourth. Jungle Cat was then off the track until late September when, on the first of the Group 1 outings in Australia, he short-headed Dollar

For Dollar in the Sir Rupert Clarke Invitation Stakes over seven furlongs. The mile was perhaps to blame for his disappointing performance next time, but then be bounced back over six furlongs to force a dead-heat with Pierata for third in the Group 1 VRC Sprint Classic at Flemington, just a neck and one and a half lengths behind Santa Ana Lane and In Her Time, and with Redzel three-parts of a length back in fifth.

Jungle Cat is one of nine Group 1 stars for Darley's notable international sire Iffraaj (by Zafonic), a horse who himself did not even earn any blacktype until he was four years old. He took the Group 2 Park Stakes over seven furlongs at Goodwood that year, repeated the feat at five, added the Group 2 Lennox Stakes at Goodwood, and failed narrowly to beat Les Arcs in the Group 1 July Cup. He stands at Dalham Hall Stud, his four-time Group 1-winning miler Ribchester is standing his second season at Kildangan Stud in 2019, and his son Wootton Bassett came up with classic star and young fellow Haras d'Etreham-based stallion Almanzor from his first crop. Iffraaj also has the Group 1-placed, Group 2-winning sprinter Hot Streak at stud (Tweenhills Farm & Stud) and that chestnut's first crop made up to 220,000gns at the yearling sales in 2018.

All of this augurs well for the prospects of Jungle Cat who, like mile Group 1 star Rizeena, is out of a mare from the Storm Cat (by Storm Bird) line.

His siblings include the dual Grade 3-placed six-figure earner Texas Wildcatter (by Monarchos), and his dam is Mike's Wildcat (by Forest Wildcat), a lightly raced and speedy juvenile stakes winner whose blacktype-placed dam, Mistyray (by In Reality), won seven times from two to four years of age. There are some blacktype horses in the next generation of the pedigree, including Mistyray's listed-winning half-sister Speier's Hope (by Minnesota Mac) and a pair of South American graded scorers, but it would seem fair to say that Jungle Cat is the best horse the family has produced in some time and that Iffraaj upgraded the page.

Jungle Cat looks likely to get some speedy and precocious juveniles – as he was at that age – and to become a source of sprinters and milers. The contribution of the mares will likely be influential in how many he can get who win over 10 furlongs, and it would be no surprise to see him get one or more classic runners in not too distant future.

SUMMARY DETAILS

Standing: Kildangan Stud, Co Kildare
Fee: €8,000
Career highlights: 8 wins inc Al Quoz Sprint (Gr1), Sir Rupert Clarke Invitation Stakes (Gr1), Al Fahidi Fort Stakes (Gr2), 2nd Gimcrack Stakes (Gr2), July Stakes (Gr2), Palace House Stakes (Gr3), Meydan Sprint (Gr3-twice), Criterion Stakes (Gr3), City Plate Stakes (L), 3rd VRC Sprint Classic (Gr1), Coventry Stakes (Gr2), Richmond Stakes (Gr2)
Other stallions by his sire include: Wootton Bassett (Gr1), Benvenue (2yo of 2019), Hot Streak (2yo), Biraaj (yearlings), Ribchester (foals)

JUNGLE CAT (IRE) - bay 2012

Iffraaj (GB)	Zafonic (USA)	Gone West (USA)
		Zaizafon (USA)
	Pastorale (GB)	Nureyev (USA)
		Park Appeal
Mike's Wildcat (USA)	Forest Wildcat (USA)	Storm Cat (USA)
		Victoria Beauty (USA)
	Old Flame (USA)	Black Tie Affair
		Mistyray (USA)

KESSAAR (IRE)

There has been a disturbing recent trend to retire colts to stud at the end of their two-year-old season before they have truly proven themselves as racehorses. Being talented at two is good, although not by any means an essential quality for a top stallion but the real competition, the most challenging tests of a racehorse come in their three-year-old season and beyond. Kessaar, a late April foal, will have completed a large chunk of his first term at stud before he even reaches his physical third birthday.

A good-looking horse who made 100,000gns as a yearling, he has returned to the stud where he was bred and where his sire has held court for many years. He was trained by John Gosden, began his career with a runner-up finish in a six-furlong York maiden in mid-May, was well-beaten in the Listed Windsor Castle Stakes over five at Ascot in June, and then ran away with a six-furlong Windsor novice event at the end of July, wearing a hood for the first time. He was then unplaced in a listed contest at Ripon, and it was only in the autumn that his form rose to a high-class level. First, he won the Group 3 188Bet Casino Sirenia Stakes by two and a half lengths on the Polytrack at Kempton, then he added the Group 2 Dubai Duty Free Mill Reef Stakes by a similar margin on soft ground at Newbury before finishing fourth to Royal Meeting in the Group 1 Criterium International over seven furlongs at Chantilly in late October.

He finished the season on an official handicap mark of 113, and although he looked like an ideal candidate for the enhanced three-year-old sprint programme, the French run was to be the final one of his career, which was disappointing.

Kessaar is one of an increasing number of sons of Kodiac (by Danehill) to go to stud, and that plus his juvenile race record will likely make him a popular addition to the ranks. Kodiac was only blacktype placed, and he got his chance at stud mainly due to the exploits of his Group 1-winning three-parts brother Invincible Spirit (by Green Desert). The latter went on to become one of Europe's leading sires, he is the flag bearer at the Irish National Stud, and in addition to his double-digit tally of Group 1-winning offspring, he also has several sons who are showing promise at stud, notably the Group 1 sires Lawman and I Am Invincible and last year's notable freshman Kingman. The Kodiac stallions, on the other hand, are all at early stages of their stud careers, and it will be 2020 before the first of them have runners on the track.

Kessaar is a full-brother to the maiden and dual handicap winner Breaking Records, a Hugo Palmer-trained gelding currently rated 87, and the pair are the first two foals out of an unraced mare called Querulous (by Raven's Pass). That John Gosden had to go to $275,000 to secure her as a yearling in Saratoga testifies to her physical qualities while also hinting at the strength of her pedigree. She is out of the Group 3-placed miler Contentious (by Giant's Causeway), and that mare is a half-sister to Gone Astray (by Dixie Union), winner of the Grade 2 Ohio Derby and Grade 2 Pennsylvania Derby, both over nine furlongs. He stands at Northwest Stud in Ocala, Florida, and the standout performer among his early stakes winners is the prolific blacktype scorer Three Rules. Crowned Florida-bred Horse of the Year in 2016, that talented sprinter-miler has earned just short of $1 million in prize money.

Illicit (by Mr Prospector), the third dam of Kessaar, was unraced but is a half-sister to 2005's US three-year-old filly champion Smuggler (by Unbridled) – who won the Grade 1 Coaching Club American Oaks and Grade 1 Mother Goose Stakes – and out of Inside Information (by Private Account), who was champion older mare in the same country 10 years before. She won 14 times from two to four years of age, including the Grade 1 features Breeders' Cup Distaff, Spinster Stakes, Acorn Stakes, Ashland Stakes, Ruffian Handicap, and Shuvee Handicap, and she was a half-sister to the similarly talented Educated Risk (by Mr Prospector). That star got her top-level wins in the Top Flight Handicap and Frizette Stakes.

As we are looking at Kessaar's future stallion potential, it becomes necessary to mention two of Inside Information's sons and one of her 'uncles'. The sons are Devious (by

Danzig), who was unraced but sired winners from a handful of foals, and four-time scorer Manipulator (by Unbridled) who went on to become a notable sire in Argentina, where he has been represented by five Grade 1 stars, including mile classic winner El Moises. The 'uncle' is Educated Risk's stakes-winning full-brother Diamond whose stakes-winning progeny include the prolific Silmaril, who retired to the paddocks with over $1 million in prize money to her name.

It will be interesting to see how Kessaar fares in his second career, but there is no doubt that his combination of race record and pedigree give him the potential to sire stakes winners in all age groups, with his best likely to come in the five to 10-furlong range.

SUMMARY DETAILS

Standing: Tally-Ho Stud, Co Westmeath
Fee: €8,000
Career highlights: 3 wins inc Dubai Duty Free Mill Reef Stakes (Gr2), 188Bet Casino Sirenia Stakes (Gr3)
Other stallions by his sire include: Adaay (yearlings of 2019), Coulsty (yearlings), Kodi Bear (yearlings), Prince Of Lir (yearlings), Ardad (foals), Koropick (foals)

KESSAAR (IRE) - bay 2016

Kodiac (GB)	Danehill (USA)	Danzig (USA)
		Razyana (USA)
	Rafha	Kris
		Eljazzi
Querulous (USA)	Raven's Pass (USA)	Elusive Quality (USA)
		Ascutney (USA)
	Contentious (USA)	Giant's Causeway (USA)
		Illicit (USA)

MERCHANT NAVY (AUS)

Leading Australian sprinter Merchant Navy, who was an unbeaten listed scorer from three starts as a juvenile, was sent to Ireland to be prepared by Aidan O'Brien for a crack at the Group 1 Diamond Jubilee Stakes at Royal Ascot before the colt would then return 'down under' to begin his stallion career immediately at Coolmore Australia.

There was a possible hitch due to the weight he would have to carry in Europe. When running in the northern hemisphere, he counted as being a four-year-old as he was born before 1st January 2015. However, his actual date of birth is 14th November 2014, making him a late-season three-year-old in his native land, yet not entitled to that weight allowance when running here. So, in effect, he was carrying penalties in both his European starts, which made his performances more meritorious. Calculating that discrepancy based on what a three-year-old receives from an older horse in May and June is not the accurate way to do it as, again, he did it as a late-season three-year-old, just shy of being classed as a four-year-old in his home territory.

With this in mind, he put up an outstanding performance first time out, beating Spirit Of Valor by a length in the Group 2 Weatherbys Ireland Greenlands Stakes at the Curragh. Tasleet was another length-and-a-quarter back in third, with a neck more back to Brando in fourth, each of them receiving weight from him due to his Group 1 penalty.

His effort at Ascot was not as impressive. It was close, very close, and also quite fortunate given how the race went for the runner-up, but Merchant Navy held on by a short-head to take the Ascot feature from the French colt City Light, with American challenger Bound For Nowhere third and English runner The Tin Man fourth. Mission accomplished. There was some brief speculation about whether or not he would remain a bit longer, to take up his entry in the Group 1 Darley July Cup at Newmarket, but that soon ended. Merchant Navy went into quarantine for a return trip to Australia.

However, now he was heading home with a European top-level win to add to his six-furlong Group 1 success at Flemington, and a 126 rating from Timeform that placed him behind only Battaash (133), Harry Angel (131) and Blue Point (129) among sprinters who raced on this continent in 2018. His status was enhanced, he did it as a late-season three-year-old forced to compete as if a four-year-old, and he has no doubt caught the attention of mare owners in this part of the world too.

A listed and Group 3 scorer for trainer Ciaron Maher, he switched to Aaron Purcell and then got up on the line to take the six-furlong Group 1 Coolmore Stud Stakes at Flemington in November 2017. He was only beaten by half a length when Group 2-placed on his next start, then by a neck when third to Redkirk Warrior in the Group 1 Newmarket Handicap in March, over the course and distance of his major win.

He was bred by Chris Barnham, and although there as aspects of the distaff side of his family that won't be familiar to many here, his sire needs no introduction. Fastnet Rock (by Danehill) is one of the most successful of all the reverse-shuttle stallions and his global tally of 142 stakes winners includes 36 who have won at the highest level, including the European-trained Group 1 stars Diamondsandrubies, Fascinating Rock, Intricately, Laganore, One Master (Qatar Prix de la Foret in 2018), Qualify, Rivet, and Zhukova.

All but two of that list are fillies, Fascinating Rock is a member of the stallion team at Ballylinch Stud, and this male line got another advertisement at the Curragh this year when Urban Fox, a daughter of Australian Group 1 scorer Foxwedge (by Fastnet Rock) – who reverse-shuttled to Whitsbury Manor Stud for four seasons – sprang a surprise in the Group 1 Juddmonte Pretty Polly Stakes. Fastnet Rock also has a few other sons who have hit the Group 1 target at stud in the southern hemisphere, but as yet none could be called a sire of note, although they are still in early stages of their stallion careers.

Merchant Navy is out of the Group 1-placed, Group 3-winning sprinter Legally Bay (by Snippets) and that makes him a full-brother to Jolie Bay. Also bred by Barnham, she was a short-head winner of the Group 2 Roman Consul Stakes over six furlongs at Randwick a month before chasing home Nechita in the Group 1 Coolmore Stud Stakes over the same trip at Flemington.

Their dam is among a string of winners produced from the seven-furlong and mile scorer Decidity (by Last Tycoon), and those siblings include three of note. The prolific Bonaria (by Redoute's Choice) won the Group 1 VRC Myer Classic over a mile, Time Out (by Rory's Jester) was a six-furlong Group 3 scorer as a juvenile, and four-time sprint winner Chatoyant (by Flying Spur) made her name at stud. That mare's best are by stallions who are very familiar to those in this part of the world. Smart two-year-old Montsegur (by New Approach) won a five-and-a-half-furlong Group 3 at Caulfield and one over six furlongs at Flemington, whereas Tessera (by Medaglia d'Oro), who was stakes-placed at seven, got his best win in a five-and-a-half-furlong juvenile Group 3 contest at Rosehill.

Decidity was out of Class (by Twig Moss), which made her a half-sister to nine-furlong Group 2 scorer Classy Fella (by Kenmare) and what could be described as being a three-parts sister to 12-furlong Group 3 winner Vestey (by Last Tycoon).

It is not impossible that some of the talented future offspring of Merchant Navy will also stay that distance, although it seems likely – given his racing profile and the achievements of those most closely related to him – that he will mostly get sprinters and milers, along with some who will be effective at 10 furlongs. He already has a southern hemisphere breeding season behind him, and he will stand the northern hemisphere half of that first year at Coolmore Stud in 2019, where his fee has been set at €20,000.

SUMMARY DETAILS

Standing: Coolmore Stud, Co Tipperary
Fee: €20,000
Career highlights: 7 wins inc Diamond Jubilee Stakes (Gr1), Coolmore Stud Stakes (Gr1), Weatherbys Ireland Greenlands

Stakes (Gr2), H.D.F. McNeil Stakes (Gr3), ANZAC Day
Stakes (L), 3rd Lexus Newmarket Handicap (Gr1), Schweppes
Rubiton Stakes (Gr2)
Other stallions by his sire include: Foxwedge (Gr1), Smart
Missile (Gr1), Stryker (Gr1), Wanted (Gr1), Highly
Recommended (Gr2), Rock 'N' Pop (Gr2), Rothesay (L), Your
Song (L), Fascinating Rock (yearlings of 2019)

MERCHANT NAVY (AUS) - bay 2014

Fastnet Rock (AUS)	Danehill (USA)	Danzig (USA)
		Razyana (USA)
	Piccadilly Circus (AUS)	Royal Academy (USA)
		Gatana (AUS)
Legally Bay (AUS)	Snippets (AUS)	Lunchtime
		Easy Date (AUS)
	Decidity (AUS)	Last Tycoon
		Class (AUS)

ORDER OF ST GEORGE (IRE)

There was a time when the Gold Cup at Ascot was one of the most prestigious races of the year and a natural target for the previous year's classic stars. It was the first race at the Royal meeting to get Group 1 status when the pattern system was introduced, but the attribute required to win it – stamina – has since become something of a dirty word. That is a pity because not only are the top stayers' races an important and popular part of the racing calendar, but the shifting trend towards early speed and precocity is greatly reducing the number of stallions with the potential to sire Derby and Oaks stars plus, of course, St Leger and Cup horses.

Order Of St George is one of the best stayers of the modern era, a horse who is as effective at 12 furlongs as he is over a mile farther, and so something of a throwback to those days of old when a Derby hero would remain in training to tackle the Ascot feature, a race that, as Timeform pointed out again in their 2016 essay on this Aidan O'Brien-trained champion, does not include the word Ascot in its title (*Racehorses of 2016*, p.740).

He began his career in July of his two-year-old season, finishing fourth in a mile maiden at Leopardstown and ran away with a similar contest over the same course and distance the following month. He was runner-up to Parish Boy over a furlong less at Naas 10 days before, and it was that same colt who beat him in the Listed Eyrefield Stakes over nine furlongs at Leopardstown that October. He missed the early season classics, was short-headed by Bondi Beach on his return to action in the Group 3 Curragh Cup in late June, but then posted wide-margin wins in Her Majesty's Plate at Down Royal and the Group 3 Irish St Leger Trial Stakes at the Curragh. That seven and a half-length defeat of Sea Moon was followed by an 11-length drubbing of Agent Murphy in the Group 1 Irish St Leger.

Timeform rated him 129 that season, only 5lbs behind Horse of the Year, Derby and Arc hero Golden Horn and although the Gold Cup was the obvious target, it was hoped by some that this exciting colt might also drop back to 12 furlongs at some point.

He ran six times as a four-year-old, duly landing the Group 1 Gold Cup at Ascot, in which he beat Mizzou by three lengths. A shock half-length defeat by Wicklow Brave in the Group 1 Irish St Leger was, however, followed by what was arguably the best performance of his career to that point. Order Of St George chased home Found and Highland Reel in the Group 1 Prix de l'Arc de Triomphe over 12 furlongs at Chantilly, beaten one and three-quarter lengths and one and a half lengths, and securing for his trainer a historic one-two-three in Europe's most prestigious race. He was favourite for the Group 2 Qipco British Champions Long Distance Cup, over two miles at Ascot, 13 days later but, on this occasion, he disappointed, finishing only fourth to Sheikhzayedroad.

His five starts in 2017 yielded three wins and two seconds, and having been short-headed by Big Orange in the Gold Cup and easily beat Rekindling when taking a third edition of the Group 3 Irish St Leger Trial at the Curragh, he went into that year's Group 1 Qatar Prix de l'Arc de Triomphe off the back of a nine-length score in the previous month's Group 1 Comer Group International Irish St Leger. It was another fine performance, this time a five-and-a-quarter-length fourth to Enable. Three weeks later, he beat Torcedor by half a length to take the Group 2 Qipco British Champions Long Distance Cup.

His six-year-old campaign started well, with a five-and-a-half-length score in the Group 3 Vintage Crop Stakes at Navan and the listed success on fast ground at Leopardstown, but he was not seen out again after his four-length fourth to Stradivarius in the Group 1 Gold Cup. It was later announced that he would take up stallion duties as a member of Coolmore's National Hunt team in 2019. His specific base was later confirmed as being their Castlehyde Stud, where the roster is made up of a mixture of flat and dual-purpose sires.

Order Of St George is among 75 Group 1 winners sired by Coolmore Stud's prolific champion sire Galileo (by Sadler's

Wells). He is a $550,000 graduate of the Keeneland September Yearling Sale and, as that fact might suggest, he comes from a top US family, which is part of why it would be fascinating to see how he might fare if given a chance as a flat sire.

He is the best of four stakes winners out of Another Storm (by Gone West), those siblings include the mile Group/Grade 3 scorers Angel Terrace (by Ghostzapper) and Asperity (by War Chant), and his dam is a daughter of 1996's US juvenile filly champion Storm Song (by Summer Squall). She won the Grade 2 Adirondack Stakes, Grade 1 Frizette Stakes and Grade 1 Breeders' Cup Juvenile Fillies, she is the grandam of the top Singapore mile to 10-furlong runner Better Life (by Smarty Jones), and she is a half-sister to the ill-fated Grade 2 Oak Leaf Stakes winner Diamond Omi (by Giant's Causeway). Her siblings also include the unraced Happy Tune (by A.P. Indy), who is the dam of 12-furlong Grade 3 scorer Symphony Kid (by Unbridled) and Grade 3-winning miler High Cotton (by Dixie Union).

Hum Along (by Fappiano), whose offspring included the $6.8 million yearling purchase Tasmanian Tiger (by Storm Cat), is the third dam of Order Of St George. She was only placed once as a two-year-old, but each of her next three dams was a multiple stakes winner. Minstress (by The Minstrel) was a Grade 3-placed dual listed scorer, Fleet Victress (by King Of The Tudors) won the Grade 2 Sheepshead Bay Handicap and was a track record setter over eight and a half furlongs at Belmont Park, and Countess Fleet (by Count Fleet) – the sixth dam of the newly retired Ballydoyle star – won the prestigious Milady and Vanity Handicaps, setting a new track record for nine furlongs in the latter.

On pedigree, Order Of St George had the potential to prove best in the mile-to-12-furlong range, with a chance of staying farther, and so, with the right mares, it is entirely possible that he could sire top-class performers over those distances, in addition to the stayers that he will surely get. He will, of course, attract most of his support from the National Hunt sector, and will no doubt eventually be represented by Grade 1 winners over hurdles and fences, but at a time when so many new flat recruits are good sprinters or milers, or even precocious sorts who retire too early, aiming him solely at the jumps market could be a missed opportunity.

SUMMARY DETAILS

Standing: Castlehyde Stud, Co Cork

Fee: €6,500

Career highlights: 13 wins inc Gold Cup (Gr1), Irish St Leger (Gr1-twice), British Champions Long Distance Cup (Gr2), Vintage Crop Stakes (Gr3), Irish St Leger Trial Stakes (Gr3-3 times), Savel Beg Stakes (Listed-3 times), 2nd Gold Cup (Gr1), Irish St Leger (Gr1), Curragh Cup (Gr3), Vintage Crop Stakes (Gr3), Eyrefield Stakes (Listed), 3rd Prix de l'Arc de Triomphe (Gr1)

Other stallions by his sire include: Cima De Triomphe (Gr1), Frankel (Gr1), Heliostatic (Gr1), Intello (Gr1), Nathaniel (Gr1), New Approach (Gr1), Rip Van Winkle (Gr1), Roderic O'Connor (Gr1), Ruler Of The World (Gr1), Sixties Icon (Gr1), Soldier Of Fortune (Gr1), Teofilo (Gr1), Treasure Beach (Gr1)

ORDER OF ST GEORGE (IRE) - bay 2012

Galileo (IRE)	Sadler's Wells (USA)	Northern Dancer (CAN)
		Fairy Bridge (USA)
	Urban Sea (USA)	Miswaki (USA)
		Allegretta
Another Storm (USA)	Gone West (USA)	Mr Prospector (USA)
		Secrettame (USA)
	Storm Song (USA)	Summer Squall (USA)
		Hum Along (USA)

SAXON WARRIOR (JPN)

There were many memorable aspects of the 2018 flat season, and the rivalry between Saxon Warrior and Roaring Lion was one of them. It started on their final outing of 2017 when a neck separated the pair of previously undefeated colts at the end of the Group 1 Racing Post Trophy, and Saxon Warrior made it two-nil when taking the Group 1 Qipco 2000 Guineas in style at Newmarket on his seasonal reappearance in May. He landed the classic by a length and a half from Tip Two Win, with Masar a head back in third, Elarqam another half-length away in fourth and a neck in front of Roaring Lion.

At this point, any predictions that the pair might develop a rivalry would have seemed fanciful as their careers appeared to be going in different directions. One was an unbeaten classic star with a pedigree that shouted Epsom and of whom there was talk of a Triple Crown bid, while the other had disappointed in his first two starts of the year, leading to the inevitable speculation as to whether or not he had trained on. The Group 1 Investec Derby changed all of that.

Masar, who had shown a touch of brilliance with a nine-length demolition job in the Group 3 Craven Stakes in April, stormed home to a length-and-a-half victory at Epsom, chased home by Dee Ex Bee, who outstayed Roaring Lion for third, the grey losing second place near the line. Odds-on favourite Saxon Warrior, however, never looked like winning, and although he kept going to the end, he had to settle for fourth, two and a half lengths behind the grey. Young Rascal (seventh), Kew Gardens (ninth) and Knight To Behold (11th) would later become significant players in the middle-distance division, but on the day the impression was that only the first two truly stayed the mile and a half.

The Triple Crown dream was over, but connections gave Saxon Warrior another try at the distance, and he was favourite for the Group 1 Dubai Duty Free Irish Derby at the Curragh. He was only beaten by half a length and a neck, but with all due respect to Latrobe and Rostropovich, nothing they had done before or achieved since indicated that this was anything other than an unremarkable edition of the classic. It was no surprise, therefore, to see him drop in trip for his next start.

The combination of fast ground and a good pace set by the 2016's winner Hawkbill helped to produce a fast time for the Group 1 Coral-Eclipse at Sandown in July, and the race provided viewers with an exciting finish as Roaring Lion and Saxon Warrior did battle. It was clear from around two furlongs from home that it was the three-year-olds who would fight it out, the bay went to the front, the grey caught him and inched ahead, but his rival fought back all the way. There was only a neck separating them at the post, then a gap of two and a half-lengths to the staying-on Cliffs Of Moher in third.

The pair met again six and a half weeks later, although this time Saxon Warrior disappointed. Roaring Lion won York's Group 1 Juddmonte International Stakes impressively by three and a quarter lengths from Poet's Word, with Thundering Blue – the only non-Group 1 winner in the line-up – staying on into third, a length and a quarter ahead of the Guineas star. His Irish Derby conqueror finished a never-dangerous seventh of the eight. The Group 1 Qipco Irish Champion Stakes was an obvious next target and, as at Sandown, the pair put on quite a show for the crowds. Saxon Warrior went to the front with under a quarter-mile to go and briefly looked like he might be about to even the score, but Roaring Lion caught him near the post and won by a neck. There was a gap of two and three-quarter lengths back to Deauville in third, and another length and a quarter gap to US Grade 1 scorer Athena.

The score was now four-two to Roaring Lion, with three of their six meetings having been settled by just a neck, and both colts held entries at the British Champions Weekend in late October. Sadly, a seventh encounter did not come to pass. It quickly emerged that Saxon Warrior picked up a career-ending injury at Leopardstown – what might have happened that day had this not occurred? – so he was immediately retired. He is now about to embark on a stallion career at Coolmore Stud.

Saxon Warrior's juvenile Group 1 win and classic victory were important from a pedigree point of view as they further advertised the potential of outstanding Japanese sire Deep Impact (by Sunday Silence) to have a significant influence in this part of the world. That 2000 Guineas win was not, as some said on the day, a first European classic success for the stallion because the Elie Lellouche-trained Beauty Parlour carried the famous Wildenstein colours to victory in the Group 1 Poule d'Essai des Pouliches (French 1000 Guineas) in 2012. She was then runner-up to the ill-fated Valyra in the Group 1 Prix de Diane (French Oaks). However, with the number of regally bred mares who have been sent to Deep Impact recently, especially by Coolmore, it's a fair bet that there are more to come.

Indeed, Saxon Warrior was not his only classic star of 2018, in Europe or elsewhere. Study Of Man won the Group 1 Prix du Jockey Club (French Derby), Wagnerian took the Grade 1 Tokyo Yushun (Japanese Derby), and Fierement landed the Grade 1 Kikuka Sho (Japanese St Leger).

Deep Impact, who is out of Group 1 winner Wind In Her Hair (by Alzao), has the influential Highclere (by Queen's Hussar) as his third dam. He was one of the most brilliant racehorses ever to be trained in Japan and the Timeform 134-rated, seven-time Group 1 ace, who stands at Shadai Stallion Station, has followed in the hoofprints of his dynasty-making sire by becoming one of the greatest stallions of the modern era.

His triple-digit tally of stakes winners consists mostly of horses who have won at Grade 3 level or above. A total of 39 have won at the highest level and, in addition to standouts such as Gentildonna, Kizuna, Real Steel, Tosen Stardom and Vivlos – to name just a few – they also include Prix d'Ispahan scorer A Shin Hikari, making it four Group 1 stars for him in Europe, so far.

Saxon Warrior, who was Timeform-rated 120p at two and 124 at three, is yet another top-level winner bred by Orpendale, Chelston & Wynatt, he is a full-brother to the stakes-placed Pavlenko and he is the second foal of Maybe (by

Galileo), a filly who finished a three-and-three-quarter-length fifth to Was in the Group 1 Oaks at Epsom on her only attempt beyond a mile. She had been a 10-length third to Homecoming Queen in the Group 1 1000 Guineas on her previous start – her first defeat – and won both the Group 1 Moyglare Stud Stakes and Group 2 Debutante Stakes over seven furlongs at the Curragh as a juvenile.

Maybe has the potential to produce both high-class milers and middle-distance horses, and given that he's a son of Deep Impact, there was every chance that Saxon Warrior would be the latter or both. His relationship to two Epsom classic stars boosted his prospects of staying 12 furlongs, but it was over eight and 10 that he showed his best form.

Promise To Be True, a full-sister to Maybe, was never asked to try beyond a mile, but then she only ran once as a three-year-old. At two she won the Group 3 Silver Flash Stakes over seven furlongs at Leopardstown, chased home Wuheida in the Group 1 Prix Marcel Boussac over a mile at Chantilly, and then took third behind Thunder Snow in the Group 1 Criterium International at Saint-Cloud, over seven furlongs on soft ground. There was no guarantee that she or Maybe would stay the Oaks distance, despite being Galileo and out of a stakes-winning three-parts sister to Oaks heroine Dancing Rain (by Danehill Dancer), and that's because their dam, Sumora (by Danehill), was a sprinter whose blacktype success came over five furlongs and as a two-year-old. The odds were excellent, of course, but likely to be dependant on which attribute Sumora had passed on to them. Maybe's Oaks fifth suggests that she may have got the stamina assist, and that would boost her prospects of producing offspring who can stay that trip.

Sumora and Dancing Rain are out of the unraced Indian Ridge (by Ahonoora) mare Rain Flower and, in addition to her three-quarter-length defeat of Wonder Of Wonders at Epsom in 2011, Dancing Rain also took the Group 1 Preis der Diana (German Oaks) over a furlong less on soft ground at Dusseldorf before adding victory in the Group 2 British Champions Fillies and Mares Stakes at Ascot. Originally a

€200,000 Goffs Orby Sale graduate, Dancing Rain made 4,000,000gns when sold at the Tattersalls December Mare Sale in Newmarket four years later, and her second foal is Magic Lily (by New Approach). That eight-length Newmarket debut winner was only beaten by three-quarters of a length when third to Laurens and September in the Group 1 bet365 Fillies' Mile at Newmarket but has not run since.

It may seem surprising that a pair of three-part sisters could show such different aptitudes – one a five-furlong filly and the other an Oaks star – but it is not so when you consider the mixed potential of their pedigrees.

Their dam is by a leading source of sprinter and miler speed, and she is a half-sister to two horses of particular note, one of whom is the high-class sprinter Archway (by Thatching). He won the Group 3 Greenlands Stakes and Listed Waterford Testimonial Stakes when trained by Vincent O'Brien, and the brightest stars among his offspring are Roman Arch, Grand Archway, Rose Archway, and Group 1 Melbourne Cup runner-up She's Archie – the latter trio all Group 1 winners over 12 furlongs. Roman Arch got his top-level wins at eight and 10 furlongs. Strange? No, not when you consider that Archway was a half-brother to Group 1 Derby and Group 1 Irish Champion Stakes star Dr Devious (by Ahonoora) – a three-parts brother to Rain Flower – and that their dam, Rose Of Jericho, was a daughter of dual Arc hero and noted stamina influence Alleged (by Hoist The Flag).

Former Peter Chapple-Hyam-trained ace Dr Devious died in 2017, at the age of 29, and although his overall record as a stallion was disappointing for a horse of his calibre and pedigree, he did leave us the Group 1 winners Kinnaird (Prix de l'Opera) and Collier Hill (Irish St Leger, Canadian International, Hong Kong Vase). With the support that Saxon Warrior is likely to receive at stud, there is every reason to hope that he will become a much more successful sire than Dr Devious was. His better two-year-olds are likely to be effective from mid-summer onwards and, also depending on the mares, his best representatives are likely to be successful within the broad seven-to-14-furlong range.

SUMMARY DETAILS

Standing: Coolmore Stud, Co Tipperary
Fee: €30,000
Career highlights: 4 wins inc Qipco 2000 Guineas (Gr1),
Racing Post Trophy (Gr1), Juddmonte Beresford Stakes (Gr2),
2nd Qipco Irish Champion Stakes (Gr1), Coral-Eclipse Stakes
(Gr1), 3rd Dubai Duty Free Irish Derby (Gr1)
Other stallions by his sire include: Deep Brillante (Gr3),
Danon Ballade (L), Kizuna (2yo of 2019), Real Impact (2yo),
Spielberg (2yo), Martinborough (yearlings), Mikki Isle
(yearlings), Satono Aladdin (foals)

SAXON WARRIOR (JPN) - bay 2015

Deep Impact (JPN)	Sunday Silence (USA)	Halo (USA)
		Wishing Well (USA)
	Wind In Her Hair (IRE)	Alzao (USA)
		Burghclere
Maybe (GB)	Galileo (IRE)	Sadler's Wells (USA)
		Urban Sea (USA)
	Sumora (IRE)	Danehill (USA)
		Rain Flower (IRE)

SIOUX NATION (USA)

The premature loss of Ashford Stud stallion and outstanding sire Scat Daddy (by Johannesburg) has been a considerable one, and it is hoped that some of his sons and daughters carry on his name with distinction at stud. He got his top-level winners at pretty much every distance from five furlongs to a mile and a half, something that may surprise European fans who associate him only with sprint stars like Acapulco, Caravaggio, Lady Aurelia, No Nay Never, and Sioux Nation. His South American fans, on the other hand, are very familiar with his record with top-class milers and middle-distance horses, and although the typically good Scat Daddy in North American has been seen to best effect in the seven to 10-furlong range, in 2018 he secured his place in the history books as the sire of Triple Crown hero Justify.

That brilliant but lightly raced chestnut is about to start his stallion career at the farm where his sire held court, as it the Aidan O'Brien-trained Grade 1 winner Mendelssohn, and that pair are among a double-digit tally of Scat Daddy horses who have joined the stallion ranks since the start of January 2018. The rush is on to find the one, or more, who may carry on his legacy, and already two of his sons have hit the Group 1 target. One is Coolmore Stud's aforementioned sprint star No Nay Never. His as yet undefeated son Ten Sovereigns won the Group 1 Juddmonte Middle Park Stakes at Newmarket in late September, his Land Force won the Group 2 Qatar Richmond Stakes at Goodwood, and four others from his first crop won listed races. He has made a promising start – and certainly nowhere near to the sort of super-stardom some proclaim – and his fee for 2019 is €100,000, four times what it was in 2018.

The other notable Scat Daddy stallion is Daddy Long Legs, whom Aidan O'Brien trained to win the Group 2 Royal Lodge Stakes at two and Group 2 UAE Derby at three. He stayed in training up to the age of five, was unplaced in all of his starts following that last win, and went to stud in Chile. Around half of his first crop to race have been winners, 15 won at two, and his offspring feature Grade 1 star Fallen From Heaven and dual Grade 3 scorer Atomicka. With a start like this, it was no surprise to see a major US stud secure his services, and he has joined the roster at Taylor Made Stallions in Kentucky for 2019, at a fee of $10,000.

In addition to Justify and Mendelssohn on their US roster, Coolmore also has No Nay Never, Caravaggio, and Sioux Nation on their Irish team. Like all but the Triple Crown star, the last-named was trained at Ballydoyle.

He made his debut over the minimum trip at Naas in early April of his juvenile year, finishing third, then chased home Brother Bear over a few yards short of six and a half furlongs at Leopardstown before winning his maiden, by three and three-quarter lengths, over six at the Curragh. He was then well-beaten behind Brother Bear in the Listed Marble Hill Stakes over the same course and distance, before going to Royal Ascot for a half-length victory in the Group 2 Norfolk Stakes over five furlongs. Once he added a half-length defeat of Beckford in the Group 1 Keeneland Phoenix Stakes over six at the Curragh in August, he all but booked his slot at stud.

Sioux Nation was unplaced behind U S Navy Flag in the Group 1 Juddmonte Middle Park Stakes on his final start at two – finishing the year on a Timeform rating of 115 – and he was very disappointing on his seasonal reappearance at three, finishing a well-beaten fourth to The Broghie Man in a listed sprint at Navan. He bounced back to beat Fleet Review by a length and a quarter in the Group 3 Goffs Lacken Stakes over six on fast ground at Naas in May, but only made the frame one more time in six subsequent outings. That was when a three-quarter-length third to Havana Grey in the Group 1 Derrinstown Stud Flying Five Stakes over the minimum trip at the Curragh in mid-September. The most notable effort among his unplaced runs was when fifth to old rival U S Navy Flag in the Group 1 Darley July Cup at Newmarket.

Sioux Nation is a full-brother to a winner, and he is the second foal out of a one-time scorer named Dream The Blues (by Oasis Dream). His dam won over six furlongs at Redcar in mid-October of her three-year-old season – her only start – and she is among seven winners out of the talented sprinter Catch The Blues (by Bluebird), the Group 3 Ballyogan Stakes heroine who was placed in the Group 1 Sprint Cup, the Group 3 Flying Five, and in two editions of both the Group 3 Greenlands Stakes and Group 3 Cork and Orrery Stakes. That mare's offspring include the dual listed-placed filly Colour Blue (by Holy Roman Emperor), she is the grandam of the Group 3 Prix de Cabourg winner My Catch (by Camacho) and Group 1-placed juvenile listed race scorer Vladimir (by Kheleyf), and her siblings include the Group 3 Ballyogan Stakes third Sharp Catch (by Common Grounds).

These are the highlights of the first three generations of Sioux Nation's pedigree. You will find Grade 3 scorer and fellow new Irish stallion Smooth Daddy (by Scat Daddy) under a branch of the fourth generation, and if you go back farther, you find that his fifth dam is Betty Lorraine (by Prince John). That half-sister to Kentucky Derby hero Majestic Prince (by Raise a Native) was the dam of Group 1 Prix du Jockey-Club star Caracolero (by Graustark) and grandam of Secreto (by Northern Dancer) – who won the Group 1 Derby at Epsom in 1984 – and his multiple Grade 1 Champion Hurdle-winning three-parts brother Istabraq (by Sadler's Wells).

It seems likely that Sioux Nation will prove popular in his new role, and with his racing and pedigree profile it can be expected that his best winners will come from five furlongs to a mile, with some staying a bit farther.

SUMMARY DETAILS

Standing: Castlehyde Stud, Co Cork
Fee: €12,500
Career highlights: 4 wins inc Keeneland Phoenix Stakes (Gr1), Norfolk Stakes (Gr2), Goffs Lacken Stakes (Gr3), 3rd Derrinstown Stud Flying Five Stakes (Gr1)
Other stallions by his sire include: Daddy Long Legs (Gr1), No Nay Never (Gr1), Daddy Nose Best (winners), Handsome Mike (winners), Frac Daddy (2yo of 2019), Caravaggio (foals), El Kabeir (foals)

SIOUX NATION (USA) – bay 2015

Scat Daddy (USA)	Johannesburg (USA)	Hennessy (USA)
		Myth (USA)
	Love Style (USA)	Mr Prospector (USA)
		Likeable Style (USA)
Dream The Blues (IRE)	Oasis Dream (GB)	Green Desert (USA)
		Hope (IRE)
	Catch The Blues (IRE)	Bluebird (USA)
		Dear Lorraine (FR)

SMOOTH DADDY (USA)

The race is on to try to find the successor(s) to the late and much lamented Scat Daddy (by Johannesburg), and there is a double-digit number of his sons who have started a stud career since January 2018. Those include US Triple Crown hero Justify and former Ballydoyle-based Grade 1 star Mendelssohn in Kentucky, plus Caravaggio, El Kabeir, and Sioux Nation in Ireland. The latter group also includes Smooth Daddy, and he will begin his new career at Clongiffen Stud in Co Meath, under the Compas Stallions banner.

The rush is partly fuelled by the promising results by two of his sons who have already had runners. No Nay Never notched up six stakes winners from his first juvenile crop in 2018, headed by Group 1 star Ten Sovereigns and Group 2 scorer Land Force, and in a drive to escalate the quality of his mates, his fee has soared to €100,000 in 2019. The other one is Daddy Long Legs, a dual Group 2 winner when based at Ballydoyle but subsequently disappointing in what was a four-season career on the track. He was the champion freshman sire in Chile, his first crop includes Grade 1 ace Fallen From Heaven and dual Grade 3 scorer Atomicka, and with a start like that it was no surprise to see a major US stud secure his services. He is now at Taylor Made Stallions in Kentucky.

Broadly speaking, there are two categories of Scat Daddys. One is the speedster, effective from five to seven furlongs, may stay a mile, and was likely precocious. With horses such as Acapulco, Caravaggio, Lady Aurelia, No Nay Never, and Sioux Nation having represented him in Europe, many associate the stallion with speed and precocity, with two-year-old talent. However, that is only one part of his story. There are all the others, the ones who excel from a mile and upwards, often showing their best as three-year-olds and older horses. They include middle-distance classic stars in South America, the aforementioned pair Justify and Mendelssohn, potential classic filly Skitter Scatter who won the Group 1 Moyglare Stud Stakes in 2018, and most of his good US runners.

SMOOTH DADDY (USA)

These horses may produce some talented two-year-olds and a few good sprinters if the mare passes on the speed gene, but their best prospects mostly lie in getting milers and middle-distance horses. They are unlikely to be your reliable source of Royal Ascot-type two-year-olds, but they could give you a classic contender. Justify, Mendelssohn, El Kabeir, and Smooth Daddy fall into that category.

The latter was placed a few times in the autumn of his two-year-old season, won a maiden at Gulfstream Park in late February of his three-year-old campaign, added a minor race at Saratoga in August, and then earned placings in a pair of nine-furlong Grade 3 turf contests at Saratoga and Belmont Park. He added another Grade 3 second the following May and got the best win of his career at the age of six when pipping Time Test by a nose in the Grade 3 Fort Marcy Stakes over nine furlongs at Belmont Park. This is the profile of a horse who may get mostly milers and middle-distance horses, aged three and upwards, plus some useful late-season juveniles.

Smooth Daddy is a $170,000 graduate of the Keeneland September Yearling Sale, he was trained by Tom Albertrani, and he is one of three blacktype offspring for his dam. The other two are fillies – listed scorer Prairie Charm (by Silver Charm) and stakes-placed Virgin Voyage (by Deputy Commander) – and they are out of the prolific Prairie Maiden (by Badger Land), a multiple stakes-winning miler and half-sister to an eight-and-a-half-furlong listed scorer.

His grandam, Will Patricia (by Bellypha), is a winning half-sister to the dam of Group 3 Ballyogan Stakes winner and Group 1 Sprint Cup third Catch The Blues (by Bluebird), and it is here that it becomes evident why this horse would catch the eye as a potential addition to the Irish stallion ranks. That smart sprinter is the grandam of Group 1 Phoenix Stakes winner and new Castlehyde Stud recruit Sioux Nation (by Scat Daddy). Catch The Blues's descendants also include Group 3 Prix de Cabourg scorer My Catch (by Camacho) and Group 1 Prix Morny third Vladimir (by Kheleyf), and if you go back to the fourth generation of the Smooth Daddy's pedigree, then you will find two European classic stars.

Caracolero (by Graustark), a half-brother to Smooth Daddy's stakes-placed third dam Native Lorraine (by Raise A Native), won the Group 1 Prix du Jockey Club (French Derby) in 1974, 10 years before his 'nephew' Secreto (by Northern Dancer) pipped El Gran Senor in the Group 1 Derby at Epsom, a performance that came shortly after he had finished third to Sadler's Wells in the Group 1 Irish 2000 Guineas at the Curragh. Secreto's dam Betty's Secret (by Secretariat) was also responsible for the great hurdler Istabraq (by Sadler's Wells), and her more distant descendants include US Grade 1 scorer Smooth Roller (by Hard Spun) and Italian Group 1 winner Close Conflict (by High Estate).

Smooth Daddy is an intriguing addition to the stallion population in Ireland. He is bred to sire milers and 10-furlong horses, some of whom may stay a bit farther, but being a son of Scat Daddy means that he is likely to attract sprint-bred mares, and that could boost his prospects and give him a shot at getting some speedier types too.

SUMMARY DETAILS

Standing: Clongiffen Stud, Co Meath
Fee: €5,000
Career highlights: 4 wins inc Fort Marcy Stakes (Gr3), 2nd Saranac Stakes (Gr3), Fort Marcy Stakes (Gr3), 3rd Hill Prince Stakes (Gr3), Tropical Park Derby (L)
Other stallions by his sire include: Daddy Long Legs (Gr1), No Nay Never (Gr1), Daddy Nose Best (winners), Handsome Mike (winners), Frac Daddy (2yo of 2019), Caravaggio (foals), El Kabeir (foals)

SMOOTH DADDY (USA) – bay 2011

Scat Daddy (USA)	Johannesburg (USA)	Hennessy (USA)
		Myth (USA)
	Love Style (USA)	Mr Prospector (USA)
		Likeable Style (USA)
Prairie Maiden (USA)	Badger Land (USA)	Codex (USA)
		Gimieroom (USA)
	Will Patricia (USA)	Bellypha
		Native Lorraine (USA)

U S NAVY FLAG (USA)

If asked, in mid-August 2017, to name the colt likely to end up champion two-year-old, many shortlists would have included Expert Eye, Unfortunately, or Sioux Nation. However, the one who topped the final rankings would surely not have been on anyone's list. By that time, U S Navy Flag had run seven times, beaten in his first four starts, then a Curragh maiden winner in first-time blinkers before chasing home Cardsharp in the Group 2 Arqana July Stakes at Newmarket and then taking fourth to Sioux Nation in the Group 1 Keeneland Phoenix Stakes.

Then came a transformation. Just a fortnight after his Phoenix Stakes run, the Aidan O'Brien-trained colt put up a surprisingly good performance to win the Group 3 Plusvital Round Tower Stakes by six lengths from Landshark, on ground described as yielding. It is fair to say that it was not a particularly strong race for the grade, but he could hardly have been more impressive. Even so, he was not the stable's first string in the following month's Group 1 Juddmonte Middle Park Stakes. However, Sioux Nation disappointed in sixth there, just ahead of another Ballydoyle runner, Declarationofpeace, while U S Navy Flag stayed on well to beat the other Aidan O'Brien-trained runner, Fleet Review, by half a length.

This was still not enough to put the colt at the top of the rankings, but then he beat his stable companions Mendelssohn, Seahenge, and Threeandfourpence – by two and a half lengths, two and a half lengths, and a head – in the Group 1 Darley Dewhurst Stakes at Newmarket, with old rival Cardsharp another length and a half back in fifth. He set a new juvenile course record for the distance, and Timeform raised his rating to 123, the highest figure awarded to any two-year-old that year. The runner-up advertised the form with victory in the Grade 1 Breeders' Cup Juvenile Turf over a mile at Del Mar.

With 11 races already behind him, there were grounds to doubt that there would be much, if any, improvement still to come from U S Navy Flag – which did not rule out his chance of winning a Guineas – but the pattern of his three-year-old form was somewhat like what it was at two, with a few standout efforts punctuated by below-par performances. Indeed, it is somewhat remarkable that this classic-placed, triple Group 1 star goes to stud with a record of having made the frame in fewer than 50% of his races.

Distance preference at three promised to be interesting as his pedigree gave him a chance of staying 10 furlongs, while his best juvenile form suggested that six to eight furlongs would be ideal. He was not asked to try beyond the mile.

His distant last of four in a seven-furlong listed race on heavy ground at Leopardstown in April was forgettable, especially after he followed that with a three-length fifth to Olmedo in the Group 1 Poule d'Essai des Poulains (French 2000 Guineas) on good ground at ParisLongchamp and then ran well in the Group 1 Tattersalls Irish 2000 Guineas on fast ground at the Curragh. He set a strong pace in the latter, and although he kept on when headed, he had to give best to Romanised, who won by two and a quarter lengths. Gustav Klimt was another length-and-a-quarter back in third, with Threeandfourpence fourth.

That quartet met again in the Group 1 St James's Palace Stakes at Royal Ascot, but this time only Gustav Klimt ran up to form, finishing a half-length runner-up to Without Parole, while his old rivals filled three of the last four placings. It was almost inevitable that U S Navy Flag would now drop back in trip for the Group 1 Darley July Cup, and he won that in style, beating Brando by a length and three-quarters.

Rather than stay in Europe to contest the season's other major sprints, he travelled to Australia for a crack at the massive prize on offer for The TAB Everest over six furlongs at Randwick. With the winner to earn over £3,785 million, and more than £1.2 million going to the runner-up, and generous prize money back through the field, it was a hard one to pass up for a team that is no stranger to travelling horses for major pots around the world, but this colt's trip 'down under' did not work out.

He was slowly away in The Everest, which was run on heavy ground, and whatever chance he might have of pulling back a top European sprint in those circumstances, he had little chance against the Australian horses and finished only ninth. He was also slowly away when finishing last of 14 in the Group 1 Ladbrokes Manikato Stakes over the same trip on good ground at Moonee Valley a fortnight later and then trailed home behind Santa Ana Lane in the Group 1 VRC Sprint Classic at Flemington, also over six on good ground. A stewards' report noted that he finished lame.

U S Navy Flag looks sure to be very popular in his new role as a stallion at Coolmore Stud, where he is being introduced at a fee of €25,000. Not only is he a son of War Front – the top-class Danzig (by Northern Dancer) sire whose early stallion sons include the Group 1 sires Declaration Of War and The Factor – but he is out of a Group 1-winning daughter of prolific champion sire Galileo (by Sadler's Wells).

That mare is Coolmore's top-class runner Misty For Me, the Group 1 Moyglare Stud Stakes, Group 1 Prix Marcel Boussac and Group 1 Irish 1000 Guineas heroine who trounced Midday by six lengths in the Group 1 Pretty Polly Stakes over 10 furlongs at the Curragh. He is her third foal, he is a half-brother to the US mile Grade 3 winner Cover Song (by Fastnet Rock) and a full-brother to his Timeform 121-rated fellow former Ballydoyle resident Roly Poly.

Her Group 1 wins came in the Kingdom of Bahrain Sun Chariot Stakes – in which she beat subsequent Group 1 scorer Persuasive by a length and a quarter – the Falmouth Stakes on the July Course at Newmarket – in which she beat Wuheida by one and a quarter lengths – and in the Prix Rothschild at Deauville, where she beat the sadly ill-fated Via Ravenna by a short-neck. Roly Poly was also a tough and talented juvenile who won the Group 3 Grangecon Stakes and Group 2 Duchess of Cambridge Stakes before being short-headed by Brave Anna in the Group 1 Cheveley Park Stakes.

These credentials gave U S Navy Flag a chance, on pedigree, to a high-class miler or 10-furlong horse, but these star relations are just the tip of the iceberg and there are also some promising signs on his page concerning his stallion potential.

One of the things that we look at when assessing a stallion's prospects is the presence or absence of previously or currently successful stallions in the distaff side of his family. Absence could indicate that it's a racing family only for its colts, yet does not mean he cannot succeed. Similarly, presence shows precedent and can give us an indication of what we might hope for, yet it does not guarantee success. The sires of those horses can be very influential, and of course, breeder support can be crucial.

Misty For Me is a full-sister to the Group 1 Prix Marcel Boussac winner Ballydoyle, who chased home Minding in both the Group 1 1000 Guineas and Group 1 Irish 1000 Guineas of 2016, and she is out of Butterfly Cove (by Storm Cat), who is an unraced half-sister to the unbeaten juvenile Group 1 sprint star Fasliyev (by Nureyev). He compiled a respectable record at stud, getting stakes and pattern winners among a long list of successful runners, and the same can be said of his dam's half-brothers Desert Wine (by Damascus) and Menifee (by Harlan).

Each of those stallions got at least one winner at the highest level, each represents a different sire line, and two of them got a Group 1 scorer in Europe. They were successful without becoming notable. U S Navy Flag, of course, represents another different sire line and is by one who could be on the verge of developing long-term significance, and he looks sure to receive strong support.

He was a champion and Group 1 star at two, and in being classic-placed over a mile before taking a Group 1 over six furlongs, he shares something in common with both major sire-sons of Danzig, albeit something that has no meaning beyond mere coincidence. Green Desert, who was a pattern winner at two, chased home Dancing Brave in the 2000 Guineas at Newmarket before dropping to sprints and retiring a Group 1 star over six furlongs, whereas Danehill was third to

Nashwan in the 2000 Guineas before doing the same. With robust support likely, there is every reason to hope that U S Navy Flag can become a sire of note. Some of his offspring may do well at two, but it is as a sire of sprinters, milers, and potentially some 10-furlong horses – even the occasional mile-and-a-half one – that he seems likely to make his name at stud.

SUMMARY DETAILS

Standing: Coolmore Stud, Co Tipperary
Fee: €25,000
Career highlights: 5 wins inc Darley July Cup Stakes (Gr1), Darley Dewhurst Stakes (Gr1), Juddmonte Middle Park Stakes (Gr1), Plusvital Round Tower Stakes (Gr3), 2nd Tattersalls Irish 2000 Guineas (Gr1), Arqana July Stakes (Gr2), 3rd Cold Move Irish EBF Marble Hill Stakes (L)
Other stallions by his sire include: Declaration Of War (Gr1), The Factor (Gr1), State Of Play (Gr2), Data Link (L), Soldat (L), War Command (L), Due Diligence (2yo of 2019), Jack Milton (2yo), Summer Front (2yo), Air Force Blue (yearlings), Hit It A Bomb (yearlings), War Correspondent (yearlings), War Dancer (yearlings), American Patriot (foals)

U S NAVY FLAG (IRE) - bay 2015

War Front (USA)	Danzig (USA)	Northern Dancer (CAN)
		Pas De Nom (USA)
	Starry Dreamer (USA)	Rubiano (USA)
		Lara's Star (USA)
Misty For Me (IRE)	Galileo (IRE)	Sadler's Wells (USA)
		Urban Sea (USA)
	Butterfly Cove (USA)	Storm Cat (USA)
		Mr P's Princess (USA)

UNITED KINGDOM

CRACKSMAN (GB)

Timeform 147-rated superstar Frankel (by Galileo) has been bred to some of the world's elite broodmares and, with such support, anything less than a plethora of stakes and pattern winners from the resulting offspring would be disappointing.

So far, 35 members of his first two crops have been stakes winners and most of them successful at least once in pattern company. January 2019's Meydan Group 3 Singspiel Stakes winner Dream Castle and Hong Kong Group 3 handicap scorer Simply Brilliant are the most recent additions to the list. His third crop includes the Kevin Ryan-trained Group 3 Prix Thomas Bryon winner and Grade 1 Breeders' Cup Juvenile Fillies Turf runner-up East. He has a champion and classic winner in Japan, colts who have been placed in the Derby at Epsom and Irish Derby (two) at the Curragh, a total of five individual Group 1 winners, and a Timeform 136-rated standout. The latter is a long way clear of the best of the stallion's other representatives, so far, which is a little surprising, given how many blacktype scorers there have been.

That star is, of course, Anthony Oppenheimer's homebred Cracksman, dual wide-margin winner of the Group 1 Qipco Champion Stakes at Ascot and, at the time of writing, rated the joint-top horse in the world, with the great Australian champion Winx, on official handicap figures.

The colt won a mile maiden at Newmarket on his only start at two, and short-headed the ill-fated Permian in a 10-furlong conditions race at Epsom a few weeks before finishing third – as favourite – to Wings Of Eagles and Cliffs Of Moher in the Group 1 Investec Derby, beaten three-quarters of a length and a neck. He looked an unlucky loser when a neck runner-up to Capri in the Group 1 Dubai Duty Free Irish Derby, but then began his sequence of impressive wins.

He powered away from Venice Beach to take the Group 2 Betway Great Voltigeur Stakes by six lengths at York, followed that with a three-and-a-half-length defeat of Avilius in the Group 2 Qatar Prix Niel at Chantilly, and then put up that memorable performance at Ascot, thrashing Poet's Word by seven lengths in the Group 1 Qipco Champion Stakes and pushing his Timeform rating to 136.

He looked as good as ever when easily taking the Group 1 Prix Ganay over 10 and a half furlongs at ParisLongchamp on his seasonal reappearance in April 2018, generating a sense of eager anticipation of a potential clash with his brilliant stable-companion Enable at some point in the year, and likely in the Arc. The Group 1 Investec Coronation Cup was his next stop, but although he won it was a disappointing effort for many. He had to fight to beat Salouen by a head – a well-exposed colt who has never won a stakes race. It emerged, however, that he had hit his head coming out of the stalls and so had likely been running a bit dazed.

He was back in action 19 days later, sent off odds-on (as on all of his starts in 2018) for the Group 1 Prince of Wales's Stakes at Royal Ascot. The ground was perhaps a little quicker than ideal for him, he did not appear to be travelling well during part of the race, and it was reported that he had been quite distracted by some fillies beforehand. Whether his mind was elsewhere or he was just on an off day is open to speculation, but old rival Poet's Word beat him by two and a quarter lengths. The winner went on to confirm his position as a top-class colt with victory in the Group 1 King George VI and Queen Elizabeth Stakes the following month, and it should be noted that the third and fourth on that day in June were Hawkbill and Cliffs Of Moher, and they finished eight lengths and another three-parts of a length behind Cracksman.

There was quite an array of negative comments about the colt on social media. What might those have been had Poet's Word not run that day? Then Cracksman could have been an easy winner of the race and likely heaped with praise, despite his antics before and during the race. But it matters not as he returned to action one more time and, sporting blinkers to help him to concentrate, he swept into the lead about a quarter-mile from home and stormed clear to beat Crystal Ocean by six lengths in the Group 1 Qipco Champion Stakes, a margin that could have been a little wider had Frankie

Dettori not eased off to wave his whip in celebration in the last half-furlong. His retirement from racing was quickly announced, although the location of his new stallion career was not revealed until later.

Cracksman is a half-brother to the Group 3 Solario Stakes winner Fantastic Moon (by Dalakhani), and he is the fourth foal out of Rhadegunda (by Pivotal), a triple winner whose tally includes the Listed Prix Solitude over nine furlongs on heavy ground at Fontainebleau, the final start in a nine-race career for the John Gosden-trained bay. Her half-brother Halla San (by Halling) earned his blacktype with third-place finishes in 14-furlong listed contests at Nottingham and York, and he was beaten by just a head when runner-up in the two-mile Northumberland Plate before going on to some success over hurdles.

His stamina stands out in contrast to the aptitude of his sister, to his dam's Listed Sirenia Stakes-winning half-brother Art Of War (by Machiavellian), and the classic speed of his grandam, On The House (by Be My Guest), the Group 1 1000 Guineas and Group 1 Sussex Stakes heroine of 1982. That Timeform 125-rated star is also the grandam of Group 2 Royal Lodge Stakes winner Leo (by Pivotal) and of dual Italian listed scorer Balkenhol (by Polar Falcon), and she is the third dam of Irish Field (by Dubawi), who won the Group 2 Prix Robert Papin and was runner-up in the Group 3 Prix du Bois.

Regarding optimal distance, Cracksman could have gone either way – miler or middle-distance horse. These first three generations are mostly about talent at up to nine furlongs, with Halla San an exception. That gelding, however, is by a stallion often noted for getting horses who excel from 12 furlongs to two miles, and so one could argue that this was the source of his stamina.

Frankel was bred to stay a mile and a half – something his triple Group 1-winning full-brother Noble Mission did – and so, with the right mares, it was always going to happen that some of his offspring would also be suited to that trip, and a bit farther. Moreover, we are seeing his stakes winners coming over a wide range of distances, from sprints up to the Cup races.

Cracksman is not the first member of his extended family to achieve hit the top over middle-distances. That's because his fourth dam is Lora (by Lorenzaccio), the unraced grandam of Nuryana (by Nureyev) and Littlewick (by Green Desert). The latter is the dam of the Chilean-bred Grade 1 Premio St Leger heroine Fontanella Borghese (by Roy), but in addition to being the stakes-winning dam of Group 1 Coronation Stakes winner Rebecca Sharp (by Machiavellian), Nuryana is a half-sister to 11-and-a-half-furlong Group 3 scorer and Derby sixth Mystic Knight (by Caerleon) and grandam of Golden Horn (by Cape Cross).

That Oppenheimer-bred, Timeform 134-rated champion won the Group 1 Derby, Group 1 Coral-Eclipse, Group 1 Irish Champion Stakes, and Group 1 Prix de l'Arc de Triomphe in 2015, he stands at Dalham Hall Stud, is a freshman sire of 2019, and his first yearlings have proved very popular in the auction ring. His string of six-figure lots includes a colt who made 550,000gns from Book 1 of the Tattersalls October Yearling Sale. Of course, his relationship to Crackman is remote, as are that of Nuryana, Fontanella Borghese, New Zealand-bred dual Group 1 mile star Obsession (by Bachelor Duke; grandam a half-sister to Nuryana), and Australian Group 1 scorers Kidnapped (by Viscount) and Hauraki (by Reset; their grandam is another half-sister to Nuryana).

Cracksman lived up to the star potential he first showed at York and went on to become the best horse that his immediate and broad family has produced. He has now been retired to stand at Dalham Hall Stud in Newmarket, at a fee of £25,000, and he looks sure to prove very popular in that new role. We can expect his offspring to prove effective from a mile and upwards, with some of them showing talent in the latter half of their juvenile year.

SUMMARY DETAILS

Standing: Dalham Hall Stud, Newmarket

Fee: £25,000

Career highlights: 8 wins inc Qipco Champion Stakes (Gr1-twice), Investec Coronation Cup (Gr1), Prix Ganay (Gr1), Qatar Prix Niel (Gr2), Betway Great Voltigeur Stakes (Gr2), 2nd Prince of Wales's Stakes (Gr1), Dubai Duty Free Irish Derby (Gr1), 3rd Investec Derby (Gr1)

Other stallions by his sire include: Cunco (southern hemisphere foals in 2019)

CRACKSMAN (GB) – bay 2014

Frankel (GB)	Galileo (IRE)	Sadler's Wells (USA)
		Urban Sea (USA)
	Kind (IRE)	Danehill (USA)
		Rainbow Lake (GB)
Rhadegunda (GB)	Pivotal (GB)	Polar Falcon (USA)
		Fearless Revival
	St Radegund (GB)	Green Desert (USA)
		On The House

DYLAN MOUTH (IRE)

There has been an increasing number of National Hunt graded winners representing the Danehill (by Danzig) sire line in recent years, and although it lags some way behind the mighty Sadler's Wells (by Northern Dancer) one, it is proving effective in that sector. Dylan Mouth, a son of Irish Derby and Prix de l'Arc de Triomphe hero Dylan Thomas (by Danehill), is one of its latest recruits. He was a middle-distance Group 1 winner and classic scorer in Italy, won a 14-furlong Group 3 contest in England last summer, and he begins his new career at Worsall Grange Stud in Yorkshire.

He is a half-brother to a pair of listed winners in Italy, the more notable of whom is Group 2 Derby Italiano runner-up Henry Mouth (by Henrythenavigator), and he is among five successful offspring of the prolific and talented Cottonmouth. All dozen of her wins came in Italy, and they included the Group 3 Premio Verziere over 10 furlongs on soft ground at San Siro plus listed contests at three different tracks.

She is a daughter of the top-class miler Noverre (by Rahy), and she is the best flat winner out of one-time juvenile scorer Nafzira (by Darshaan). Her siblings include a horse who won a couple of races in Hong Kong, but she is also a half-sister to two hurdlers of note, and that is likely to add to her son's appeal with National Hunt breeders. French breeding is all the rage in the jumping world, and quite a few of their stallions were themselves at least capable performers over hurdles or fences. If you can't breed to such a horse, then why not to a tough, prolific and high-class one who is closely related to some good hurdlers?

Roconga (by Rakti) – who has won twice over middle-distances on the flat, and represents the Danzig (by Northern Dancer) sire line – was a five-length winner of a blacktype handicap hurdle at Killarney in the summer of 2016. Jumbo Rio (by Captain Rio), on the other hand, was rated a useful 93 on the flat but excelled over obstacles and got his best win when taking the Grade 1 Ballymore Champion Four Year Old

Hurdle over two miles at Punchestown 10 years ago. He also won the Grade 2 Spring Juvenile Hurdle at Leopardstown and the Grade 3 Grimes Hurdle at Tipperary, and he was trained by Edward O'Grady.

Nafzawa (by Green Dancer), the third dam of Dylan Mouth, earned her blacktype when finishing third in the Listed Radley Stakes at Newbury as a two-year-old. She, in turn, is out of a half-sister to 1998's Grade 1 Arkle Challenge Trophy Chase star Champleve (by Kendor) and Grade 1-placed, US Grade 3 winner Nediym (by Shareef Dancer), and her grandam is a half-sister to the dam of runaway and ill-fated Group 1 Derby hero Shergar (by Great Nephew). If you go even farther back, then you will find that Dylan Mouth is a direct descendant of 1959's Poule d'Essai des Pouliche winner Ginetta (by Tulyar), whose fourth dam was the brilliant Mumtaz Mahal (by The Tetrarch). That has no bearing on his potential as a stallion, of course, but it caught the eye.

It seems unlikely that Dylan Mouth will have more than a handful of runners on the flat, but there is every reason to hope that he can do well as a sire of point-to-pointers, bumper horses, hurdlers, and chasers. It will be interesting to see the range in which they prove effective, but given that he won a pattern race over 14 furlongs last year and is related to some talented National Hunt horses, it is possible that at least some of his offspring will be effective at three miles and above.

SUMMARY DETAILS

Standing: Worsall Grange Stud, Yorkshire
Fee: £2,000
Career highlights: 14 wins inc Premio Roma (Gr1), Gran Premio di Milano (Gr1), Gran Premio del Jockey Club (Gr1), Derby Italiano (Gr2), Premio Federico Tesio (Gr2-twice), Gran Premio di Milano (Gr2), Silver Cup Stakes (Gr3), Premio Carlo d'Alessio (Gr3), Premio Emanuele Filiberto (L), 2nd Gran Premio del Jockey Club (Gr1), Fred Archer Stakes (L), 3rd Floodlit Stakes (L)
Other stallions by his sire include: Pether's Moon (2yo of 2019)

DYLAN MOUTH (IRE) – bay 2011

Dylan Thomas (IRE)	Danehill (USA)	Danzig (USA)
		Razyana (USA)
	Lagrion (USA)	Diesis
		Wrap It Up
Cottonmouth (IRE)	Noverre (USA)	Rahy (USA)
		Danseur Fabuleux (USA)
	Nafzira (IRE)	Darshaan
		Nafzawa (USA)

EXPERT EYE (GB)

With so much hype and focus every year on young and largely unproven stallion prospects who peaked in their two-year-old season – horses who may sparkle for their first two or three years at stud before fizzling out – it is good to see that reliable veterans who continue to get good horses without challenging for championship honours not only retain support but build their profile in their later years. Acclamation (by Royal Applause) is a good example, and such has been the way the market views sprinters these days he may have struggled if he was retiring to stud now, especially having an unfashionable pedigree.

He won three of his five starts at two, including a sales race, and he was listed placed, but he ran only twice at three and had added just a conditions race by August of his four-year-old season, and that was in a dead-heat. It was after that win that his best form emerged – a third-place finish to Oasis Dream in the Group 1 Nunthorpe Stakes, listed success at Goodwood, victory in the Group 2 Diadem Stakes at Ascot, then fourth to Patavellian in the Group 1 Prix de l'Abbaye de Longchamp. He has spent his stallion career at Rathbarry Stud, has risen from an initial €10,000 fee to the €40,000 he will command in 2019 – his 16th season – and he now has five Group 1 winners to his name, two of whom are stallions of note and two of whom look likely to earn that description in the not too distant future. The fifth one is his Nunthorpe Stakes and Prix de l'Abbaye heroine Marsha.

He and his hugely popular son Dark Angel have sired 49 stakes winners apiece, and counting, with the latter being responsible for the top-level stars Battash, Harry Angel, Hunt, Lethal Force, Mecca's Angel, Persuasive, and December 2018's Grade 1 Hollywood Derby scorer Raging Bull. Equiano's double-digit tally of stakes winners is headed by triple Group 1 standout The Tin Man, whereas Aclaim covered 160 mares in his first season at the National Stud in Newmarket, so has a large initial crop due to arrive in the coming months.

All of this augurs well for the prospects of the fourth top-level-winning son of Acclamation, Grade 1 Breeders' Cup Mile hero Expert Eye. The Juddmonte homebred has joined the small but mighty stallion team at Banstead Manor Stud in Newmarket, to stand alongside the established duo Frankel and Oasis Dream, rising star Kingman, and blacktype-sire Bated Breath, son of the now retired long-time team member Dansili.

Expert Eye was trained by Sir Michael Stoute and he wasted no time in advertising his star potential, kicking off his career with an eye-catching debut win over six and a half furlongs at Newbury in mid-June of his juvenile year and then putting up a performance in the Group 2 Qatar Vintage Stakes that was both visually exciting and good on the clock. He took up the running more than a quarter-mile from home and dismissed Zaman, Mildenberger, James Garfield and Seahenge by four and a half lengths and more. Although a big disappointment when coming home last behind U S Navy Flag in the Group 1 Darley Dewhurst Stakes on his final outing, he went into winter quarters with a Timeform rating of 117p, a figure he raised to 124 by the end of this year.

He was beaten by three-quarters of a length by James Garfield in the Group 3 Al Basti Equiworld Supporting Greatwood Greenham Stakes at Newbury on his seasonal reappearance, having pipped Hey Gaman – a neck runner-up in the Group 1 Poule d'Essai des Poulains (French 2000 Guineas) next time – on the line. It was even more disappointing when he finished down the field behind Saxon Warrior in the Group 1 Qipco 2000 Guineas a fortnight later. However, he stormed home by four and a half lengths in the Group 3 Jersey Stakes at Royal Ascot, chased home Lightning Spear in the Group 1 Qatar Sussex Stakes at Goodwood, and beat Gordon Lord Byron by a length and a quarter in the Group 3 Sky Bet City of York Stakes in late August.

The latter and the Ascot race are over seven furlongs, but he returned to a mile for his final two starts. He didn't have the clearest of runs in the Group 1 Prix du Moulin de Longchamp at ParisLongchamp in early September but stayed on well to take third to Recoletos and Wind Chimes, beaten a head and one and a quarter lengths. Two months later he guaranteed his future stallion career with victory in the Grade 1 Breeders' Cup Mile at Churchill Downs, again staying on well in the final furlong. He won by half a length from Catapult with a trio flashing past the post together just a neck behind, and the previous month's Group 1 Prix de la Foret heroine One Master coming off worst in that photo, having to settle for fifth place.

There was some speculation afterwards as to what the 2019 plans would be for Expert Eye as, if he remained in training, he looked a natural candidate for races such as the Group 1 Juddmonte Lockinge Stakes, Group 1 Queen Anne Stakes and Group 1 Qatar Sussex Stakes. However, the decision came quite soon, and he looks sure to be a very busy member of the Banstead Manor team, especially with a starting fee of £20,000. Might he be a future mate for Enable? It would be an interesting cross.

Although Acclamation tends to be associated with sprinters, there is no surprise that this star son excelled over a mile. He is a half-brother to a mile winner, he's out of Exemplify (by Dansili), who is a mile-winning half-sister to Group 1 1000 Guineas and Group 1 Poule d'Essai des Pouliches (French 1000 Guineas) scorer Special Duty (by Hennessy), and related to a string of horses who achieved fame at a mile and upwards.

Special Duty, who also won the Group 1 Cheveley Park Stakes over six furlongs at two, had the unusual although not unique distinction of having got two of her Group 1 wins in the stewards' room. She lost out narrowly in photo finishes for both the 1000 Guineas and Poule d'Essai des Pouliches, but Jacqueline Quest (Line of Duty's dam) was dropped to second at Newmarket, Liliside to sixth at Longchamp, and Juddmonte's filly got both races. In 2001, Vahorimix was awarded both the Poule d'Essai des Poulains and Prix Jacques le Marois after Noverre failed the post-race test at Longchamp and Proudwings was thrown out at Deauville for interference caused.

Quest For Peak (by Distant View), the grandam of Expert Eye, is out of the pattern-placed dual stakes winner Viviana (by Nureyev) and that makes her both a full-sister to seven-time Grade 1 heroine Sightseek and half-sister to dual Grade 1 scorer Tates Creek (by Rahy), a pair of Bobby Frankel-trained Juddmonte-bred standouts. Sightseek's blacktype-placed son Raison D'Etat (by A.P. Indy) stands at Calumet Farm in Kentucky and has sired winners from a small number of early runners.

Viviana's winning full-sister Willstar has produced two blacktype winners and is the grandam of several blacktype earners – the latter group featuring Group 3 Prix de Fontainebleau winner Glaswegian (by Selkirk) and dual listed scorer Preferential (by Dansili) – but the standout among them all is her excellent daughter Etoile Montante (by Miswaki). Runner-up in the Group 1 Prix Marcel Boussac as a juvenile, she was third in the Group 1 Poule d'Essai des Pouliches, took second in the Group 1 Prix Maurice de Gheest and then won the Group 1 Prix de la Foret before crossing the Atlantic where, at the age of four, she added the Grade 2 Palomar Handicap and Grade 3 Las Cienegas Handicap and finished runner-up in the Grade 1 Matriarch Stakes. Etoile Montante, another Juddmonte homebred, died at the age of 15, but her offspring include Starformer (by Dynaformer), who was Group 3-placed at Longchamp before going to the USA where she won the Grade 2 New York Stakes over 10 furlongs at Belmont Park and a trio of Grade 3 contests at 11-12 furlongs.

Viviana and Willstar are half-sisters to the Grade 1-placed Grade 2 scorer Revasser (by Riverman) and Grade 1-placed stakes winner Hometown Queen (by Pleasant Colony), the latter being the dam of Grade 2 winner and successful sire Bowman's Band (by Dixieland Band). They are out of Nijinsky Star (by Nijinsky), an unraced daughter of triple Grade 1-winning standout Chris Evert (by Swoons Son) and so are related to a host of talented horses, including Grade/Group 1 stars Chief's Crown (by Danzig), Classic Crown (by Mr Prospector), Excellent Art (by Pivotal) and Winning Colors (by Caro). The latter famously beat the colts to take the

Kentucky Derby in 1988. Chief's Crown's 47 stakes winners included seven who won at the highest level, notably Grand Lodge whose dozen Group 1-winning offspring featured the late Arc and dual Derby hero – and classic sire – Sinndar.

With family connections like these, it is clear why Expert Eye was effective over slightly farther than are many by his sire, and his combination of pedigree, performance and expected breeder support also give him every chance of becoming another notable sire son of Acclamation.

SUMMARY DETAILS

Standing: Banstead Manor Stud, Newmarket
Fee: £20,000
Career highlights: 5 wins inc Breeders' Cup Mile (Gr1), Qatar Vintage Stakes (Gr2), Sky Bet City of York Stakes (Gr3), Jersey Stakes (Gr3), 2nd Qatar Sussex Stakes (Gr1), Al Basti Equiworld Supporting Greatwood Greenham Stakes (Gr3), 3rd Prix du Moulin de Longchamp (Gr1)
Other stallions by his sire include: Dark Angel (Gr1), Equiano (Gr1), Harbour Watch (Gr2), Lilbourne Lad (Gr3), Mehmas (yearlings in 2019), Aclaim (foals), Attendu (foals)

EXPERT EYE (GB) – bay 2015

Acclamation (GB)	Royal Applause (GB)	Waajib
		Flying Melody
	Princess Athena	Ahonoora
		Shopping Wise
Exemplify (GB)	Dansili (GB)	Danehill (USA)
		Hasili (IRE)
	Quest To Peak (USA)	Distant View (USA)
		Viviana (USA)

HARBOUR LAW (GB)

There were 46 individual Group/Grade 1 winners among a career total of 198 blacktype scorers by the great stallion Danzig (by Northern Dancer), and although many of his stallion sons got at least one top-level winner of their own at stud, there are only two who have forged their powerful branch of his line: Danehill and Green Desert. The latter's stallion sons feature the Group 1-winning sprinter Invincible Spirit, who stands at the Irish National Stud, and there is a growing number of that horse's sons getting stakes and pattern winners of their own.

French classic star Lawman was one of Invincible Spirit's first sons to go to stud, and although his overall tally of 30 stakes winners is decent yet unremarkable, five of that number have won at the highest level, and two of those are classic stars. Group 1 St James's Palace Stakes winner Most Improved represents his first crop, and although given a berth at stud, he has not yet sired anything of note. Group 1 Irish 1000 Guineas heroine Just The Judge, who went on to add the Grade 1 E P Taylor Stakes, came from his second crop, as did the Group 1 Gran Criterium scorer Law Enforcement (aka Rocket Fly).

When Marcel won the Group 1 Racing Post Trophy at Doncaster, many fans thought that there could be a Lawman-sired classic star from among his fifth crop. There is, but it is not that Peter Chapple-Hyam trained bay. Marcel was among the market leaders for the Group 1 2000 Guineas at Newmarket but performed a long way below expectations, coming home last behind Galileo Gold. The colt was not seen out again but retired to the National Stud in Newmarket. Those in his small first crop are now yearlings.

The day after that classic defeat, another member of the crop won a 12-furlong Salisbury maiden, an event of no apparent significance. It was his first start for the Epsom-based Laura Mongan team, he had been runner-up in a similar contest over 12 furlongs on the artificial track at Lingfield on his debut in mid-March, and he followed-up in a 14-furlong handicap at Sandown before finishing a three-quarter-length runner-up to Sword Fighter in the Listed Queen's Vase over two miles at Royal Ascot. A few weeks later he finished fourth to Housesofparliament in the Group 3 Bahrain Trophy over 13 furlongs at Newmarket – clearly talented but without making an impact on the racing public's consciousness. However, then he went on to earn his place in the history books.

The 2016 Group 1 Ladbrokes St Leger was quite a dramatic renewal. Idaho, who had been dual classic-placed before beating the aforementioned Housesofparliament impressively in the Group 2 Great Voltigeur Stakes at York, stumbled and unseated his rider about three furlongs from home. His stable companion and York victim looked set for glory when sweeping to the front over two out but then got into a duel with Ventura Storm. A furlong out, the Richard Hannon-trained bay appeared to be getting the better of the Aidan O'Brien-trained chestnut, with 22/1 Harbour Law looking likely to take an honourable but probably soon forgotten third. The Ballydoyle colt fought back and narrowed the deficit to inches, but Harbour Law also stayed on strongly. The George Baker-ridden colt hit the front shortly before the line and went away to win by three-parts of a length. There was a short-head between second and third, and the first three finished 10 lengths clear of the fourth.

Like the previous year's Derby and Arc hero Golden Horn and recently retired dual runaway Group 1 Qipco Champion Stakes star Cracksman, Harbour Law was bred by Hascombe and Valiant Studs. He is no relation to those Timeform 134 and 136-rated champions, and he was led out unsold at 24,000gns when offered in Newmarket as a yearling. Six and a half months later he made £30,000 at the Goffs London Sale.

He stayed in training as a four-year-old, disappointed first time out in the Group 3 Henry II Stakes at Ascot, but then put up an eye-catching performance to take third in the Group 1 Gold Cup over two and a half miles at the same venue in June. This was the edition in which Big Orange and Order Of St George fought out that memorable battle, with just a short-head between them at the line, and Harbour Law came home six lengths behind the pair, with horses such as Torcedor and Sheikhzayedroad not far behind him. He looked set to make an impact on the stayers' scene, but sadly he picked up an injury that ultimately ended his track career.

Harbour Law is the fifth foal out of Abunai (by Pivotal), which makes him a half-brother to the pattern-placed gelding Moheet (by High Chaparral). His dam, who was trained by Roger Charlton, stayed seven furlongs at three but got all three of her wins as a juvenile: a five-furlong Bath maiden, a five-furlong Newmarket nursery and a six-furlong nursery on turf at Southwell. Her final two career outings were losses by a head and by a short-head, and she achieved a peak handicap mark of 85.

There is no surprise that a well-bred mare such as her could produce a Group 1 performer, although when one considers her family's profile, it would have been expected that she might get a talented miler or even middle-distance horse by Lawman rather than one who stays so well. She is a half-sister to the Grade 1 E P Taylor Stakes heroine Miss Keller (by Montjeu), to the dual 10-furlong pattern-placed gelding Sir George Turner (by Nashwan), to stakes-placed prolific scorer Tissifer (by Polish Precedent) and to Kotsi (by Nayef), who was runner-up in the Group 2 May Hill Stakes as a two-year-old and listed-placed over 10 furlongs at three.

Abunai's siblings also include two fillies who went on to success at stud. Umlilo (by Mtoto) was only placed, but her successful progeny include Fantastic Pick (by Fantastic Light), who won the Grade 2 Oak Tree Derby over nine furlongs at Hollywood Park, and the other sister of note is the one-time scorer Oshiponga (by Barathea). She is the dam of Group 2 Superlative Stakes winner Hatta Fort (by Cape Cross) and Group 3 Sweet Solera Stakes scorer Blue Bayou (by Bahamian Bounty). Oshiponga's grandson Ayaar (by Rock Of Gibraltar) won a Group 3 contest over seven furlongs at a juvenile, became a capable handicapper at around a mile, and reached a handicap mark of 102, but another of her grandsons showed more stamina than might have been expected.

Agent Murphy (by Cape Cross) is out of her unraced daughter Raskutani (by Dansili), he was a five-length winner of the Group 3 Geoffrey Freer Stakes over the extended 13 furlongs at Newbury and chased home 11-length winner Order Of St George in the Group 1 Irish St Leger, holding off the Willie Mullins-trained Wicklow Brave who was a neck back in third. That high-class dual-purpose gelding, who was 20/1 on this occasion, has developed into a leading stayer and he sprang a surprise in the same Group 1 test 12 months later.

The grandam of Harbour Law is Ingozi (by Warning), who got her listed success over a mile at Sandown. She was out of the Group 2 Child Stakes heroine and Group 1 Coronation Stakes runner-up Inchmurrin (by Lomond), and that popular filly was, in turn, a half-sister to the Group 2 Mill Reef Stakes scorer Welney (by Habitat). Ingozi's string of notable siblings includes half-sister Incheni (by Nashwan), who won the Listed Ballymacoll Stud Stakes, and half-brother Inchinor (by Ahonoora), the Group 3 Greenham Stakes and Group 3 Hungerford Stakes winner who was runner-up in the Group 1 Dewhurst Stakes at two and went on to become a successful Group 1 sire, but died aged 11. His relationship to Harbour Law adds to the interest and potential of the younger horse.

Inchmahome (by Galileo) only made the frame once in six starts, and she achieved a peak handicap mark of 66, but that sole placing was a victory in an 11-and-a-half-furlong handicap at Lingfield, and she is the dam of the talented Venus De Milo (by Duke Of Marmalade). That Aidan O'Brien-trained filly won the Listed Naas Oaks Trial over 10 furlongs, was a half-length runner-up to Chicquita in the Group 1 Irish Oaks and then an odds-on winner of the Group 3 Give Thanks Stakes at Cork before chasing home The Fugue in the Group 1 Yorkshire Oaks. She did not reach the heights at four that this early form promised, but added the Group 3 Munster Oaks at Cork, was runner-up to Thistle Bird in the Group 1 Pretty Polly Stakes at the Curragh, and third to Sultanina in the Group 1 Nassau Stakes at Goodwood.

Inchyre (by Shirley Heights), another half-sister to Ingozi, won a mile maiden at Warwick and missed out on blacktype when only fourth in listed contests over 10 and 12 furlongs on her only subsequent outings. There are, however, plenty of her descendants who have earned that value-enhancing distinction. Her son Ursa Minor (by Galileo) won the Group 3 Irish St Leger Trial Stakes over 14 furlongs at the Curragh shortly before finishing fourth behind Encke in the Group 1 St Leger at Doncaster. Inchiri (by Sadler's Wells) sprang a 25/1 surprise in the Listed Galtres Stakes at York, shortly after finishing third in a similar contest at Chepstow, and her progeny include Hawk's Eye (by Hawk Wing), who was a dual 10-furlong winner in England before becoming a blacktype performer in South Africa.

Another daughter, Inchberry (by Barathea), picked up some blacktype when a six-length runner-up in a mile listed contest at two and, although she retired a maiden – she was disqualified after passing the post in front at Hamilton as a juvenile – her performance-of-a-lifetime effort was one for which she earned no blacktype. She was only beaten by a total of two and a half lengths when fourth, at 100/1, to Casual Look in the Group 1 Oaks at Epsom. Inchberry's son Measuring Time (by Dubai Destination) was multiple Group 3-placed over middle-distances.

Inchyre is also the dam of Whirly Bird (by Nashwan), who reeled off a five-timer from nine and a half furlongs to 11 furlongs and who was listed-placed at Windsor on her final start before eventually going on to two horses of note. Her star daughter is Malabar (by Raven's Pass), the Mick Channon-trained filly won the Group 3 Prestige Stakes at two, she added a three-length score in the Group 3 Thoroughbred Stakes over a mile at Goodwood, and missed out on additional blacktype when fourth in each of the Group 1 Moyglare Stud Stakes, Group 1 Prix Marcel Boussac and Group 1 1000 Guineas. Her star son, on the other hand, is 2018's middle-distance star Poet's Word (by Poet's Voice), who was Timeform-rated 132 after completing his Group 1 Prince of Wales's Stakes - Group 1 King George VI and Queen Elizabeth Stakes double.

Despite all of this mile and middle-distance talent, there is another talented horse in the family who stayed two miles. His relationship to Harbour Law is remote, but his grandam is a full-sister to the younger colt's third dam. Balnaha, a full-sister to Inchmurrin, is best known as being the dam of the Group 1 Coronation Stakes heroine Balisada (by Kris) but, in addition to producing the 12-furlong listed scorer Galactic Star (by Galileo), that high-class miler gave us El Salvador (by Galileo). He was listed-placed a few times, including when beaten a nose by Tarana in the Listed Martin Molony Stakes over 12 and a half furlongs at Limerick, but he was also placed in the two-mile, five and a half-furlong Queen Alexandra Stakes at Royal Ascot and finished his career with victory in the two-mile Irish Cesarewitch at the Curragh in 2014.

Harbour Law is the latest high-class performer to represent a well-established blacktype-producing family, one that is usually associated with milers or middle-distance horses and is no stranger to producing Group 1 horses. It will be interesting what sort of support he gets in his new role at Batsford Stud, and it would be no surprise to see him get some high-class offspring on the flat and under National Hunt rules. He is, after all, a classic-winning relation to Inchinor and represents the Green Desert sire line.

SUMMARY DETAILS

Standing: Batsford Stud, Gloucestershire
Fee: £4,000
Career highlights: 3 wins inc Ladbrokes St Leger Stakes (Gr1), 2nd Queen's Vase (L), 3rd Gold Cup (Gr1)
Other stallions by his sire include: Most Improved (winners), Marcel (yearlings in 2019)

HARBOUR LAW (GB) – bay 2013

Lawman (FR)	Invincible Spirit (IRE)	Green Desert (USA)
		Rafha
	Laramie (USA)	Gulch (USA)
		Light The Lights (FR)
Abunai (GB)	Pivotal (GB)	Polar Falcon (USA)
		Fearless Revival
	Ingozi (GB)	Warning
		Inchmurrin

HARRY ANGEL (IRE)

The 2017 European sprinting season was lit up by a pair of three-year-olds of rare brilliance: Battaash and Harry Angel. The gelding won the Group 2 King George Stakes and Group 1 Prix de l'Abbaye and was rated 136 by Timeform. The colt, who excelled over a furlong farther, landed both the Group 1 Darley July Cup and Group 1 32Red Sprint Cup, finishing that year on a Timeform rating of 132. The news that they were to remain in training at four generated plenty of excitement, but although both produced flashes of their prodigious talent, neither added to his Group 1 haul. Battaash will presumably be back in action in 2019, but Harry Angel is now at Dalham Hall Stud in Newmarket.

It is remarkable that both stars are sons of Yeomanstown Stud stallion Dark Angel (by Acclamation), a horse who raced only at two, won the Group 1 Middle Park Stakes and was rated just 113 by Timeform. He has been a huge success for the Co Kildare-based team. A total of seven of his 49 stakes winners have stuck at least once at the highest level, and they include dual Nunthorpe Stakes heroine Mecca's Angel, July Cup and Diamond Jubilee Stakes star Lethal Force, Queen Elizabeth II Stakes winner Persuasive, and two US Grade 1 scorers: Hunt and Raging Bull.

The last three of those add a valuable extra dimension to Dark Angel's stallion profile because they are not sprinters. Persuasive was a miler, Raging Bull's top win came over nine furlongs in December, and mile star Hunt has also won a Grade 2 contest over 11 furlongs. It would be no surprise, therefore, if he was to get a Group 1 classic star some day, either over a mile or possibly even one of the 10-and-a-half-furlong French contests. Indeed, he has already given us last year's Group 1 2000 Guineas runner-up Tip Two Win.

Although unquestionably a top-class sire of racehorses, there is always a change that the unfashionably bred stallion who made it big in that way will not find a son who can carry on his legacy, and the early results for the Dark Angel stallions have been disappointing. Lethal Force's eldest are now four-year-olds but, at the time of writing, he does not have even a single stakes winner. Alhebayeb and Heeraat had adequate but unexciting results with their first juveniles in 2018, and at this point, the Group 1-placed non-stakes winner Tough As Nails, who has had limited support, has done as well as any of them. There is, however, something else to be considered. Stars may emerge from the early stock by an unfashionably bred stallion but may lack the strength of a suitable distaff line. The better prospect, therefore, may come from later crops, the products of better mares, and so that quiet early start as a sire of stallions could develop eventually into a powerful sire line. It can even happen with elite-bred stallions, that it can take a while before they start getting good sire sons.

It may seem inconceivable to those who have only come into the industry in the past decade or so, but there was a time when Danehill, Green Desert, and Sadler's Wells looked in danger of fading from prominence. The first-named was dominating in Australia of course, but it was only in the later years of the European part of his career that he became a real force here. Many of the early Green Desert and Sadler's Wells stallions were also unremarkable. Yes, the former had New Zealand champion sire Volksraad from those early days, whereas Sadler's Wells's best were In The Wings (Europe), El Prado (USA), and Fort Wood (South Africa) until Galileo and Montjeu emerged.

Could Harry Angel become one of the first notable stallion sons of Dark Angel? Yes, it is possible, and if he gets Group 1 winners, then he won't be the first in his family to achieve the feat. That said, his actual relationship to multiple Grade 1 sire Stephen Got Even (by A.P. Indy) is remote, but they share a common female ancestor, so the precedent for the family has been set.

Harry Angel took the unusual step of gaining his maiden success in the Group 2 Mill Reef Stakes. He is one of two winners out of the placed mare Beatrix Potter (by Cadeaux Genereux), he has a yearling full-sister waiting in the wings, and his two-year-old half-brother, who represents the first crop of the Showcasing (by Oasis Dream) horse Cappella Sansevero, has been named Pierre Lapin. His dam is a half-sister to the dual Hong Kong mile Group 1 star Xtension (by Xaar) – who sired three winners from a tiny first juvenile crop last year – and also to A Huge Dream (by Refuse To Bend), the stakes-placed dam of dual sprint listed scorer Mrs Gallagher (by Oasis Dream).

Great Joy (by Grand Lodge), his grandam, was a stakes-placed winner in Germany, and in addition to being a half-sister to listed scorer A La Carte (by Caerleon), her siblings include Bally Souza (by Alzao), dam of the Listed Round Tower Stakes winner and Group 1 National Stakes runner-up Wathab (by Cadeaux Genereux). It is under the next generation that the big names appear.

Third dam Cheese Soup (by Spectacular Bid) was an unraced half-sister to Lyphard's Princess (by Lyphard) – who is the stakes-winning dam of Grade 2 Ohio Derby scorer Private Man (by Private Account) – to Grade 2 winner Minneapple (by Riverman), and also to Baroness Direct (by Blushing Groom), a Grade 3 Las Flores Handicap heroine with many blacktype descendants. The aforementioned Grade 1 star and Grade 1 sire Stephen Got Even is among them, as is the multiple Grade 1-winning filly Artemis Agrotera (by Roman Ruler). The common ancestor shared by Stephen Got Even and Harry Angel is the prolific Avum (by Umbrella Fella), their third dam and fourth dam respectively.

Harry Angel was a Timeform 111p-rated juvenile and an outstanding sprinter at three and four years of age, rated 132 and 131 by that organisation at the end of those campaigns. He will surely get strong support in his new home, and there is every reason to hope that he can make an impact at stud, getting capable two-year-olds and high-class three-year-old and older horses, likely from five furlongs to a mile, with a few who may stay farther.

SUMMARY DETAILS

Standing: Dalham Hall Stud, Newmarket
Fee: £20,000

Career highlights: 5 wins inc Darley July Cup (Gr1), 32Red Sprint Cup (Gr1), Duke of York Clipper Logistics Stakes (Gr2), Armstrong Aggregates Sandy Lane Stakes (Gr2), Dubai Duty Free Mill Reef Stakes (Gr2), 2nd Commonwealth Cup (Gr1), Qipco British Champions Sprint Stakes (Gr1), Merribelle Stable Pavilion Stakes (Gr3)
Other stallions by his sire include: Alhebayeb (winners), Heeraat (winners), Lethal Force (winners), Tough As Nails (winners), Gutaifan (2yo in 2019), Estidhkaar (yearlings), Markaz (yearlings), Birchwood (foals)

HARRY ANGEL (IRE) – bay 2014

Dark Angel (IRE)	Acclamation (GB)	Royal Applause (GB)
		Princess Athena
	Midnight Angel (GB)	Machiavellian (USA)
		Night At Sea
Beatrix Potter (IRE)	Cadeaux Genereux	Young Generation
		Smarten Up
	Great Joy (IRE)	Grand Lodge (USA)
		Cheese Soup (USA)

HAVANA GREY (GB)

Like his sire before him, Galileo (by Sadler's Wells) has had an enormous influence, and there are already 14 of his sons who have sired at least one top-level winner in one of the world's Category I-listed countries. Of those, Frankel, New Approach and Teofilo have established themselves as being important stallions, and now the test of the line is to see through how many more generations the influence can extend. The latter two have a few sons at stud, and both have one who has made a promising start with his first runners. For Teofilo, that is his Group 1-winning miler Havana Gold, a member of the team at Tweenhills Farm & Stud in Gloucestershire, and now that young son has a stallion son of his own.

Havana Grey represents his first crop and could hardly have given his sire a better start as, following a five-length maiden success in early May of his two-year-old campaign, he won two of the season's earliest juvenile stakes races, then added a one-and-three-quarter-length defeat of Invincible Army in the Group 3 Molecomb Stakes before chasing home Unfortunately in the Group 1 Prix Morny – the only time he ever tried six furlongs. He rounded off that first year with a second-place finish to Group 2 Queen Mary Stakes winner Heartache in the Group 2 Flying Childers Stakes, and he went into winter quarters with a 112 Timeform rating.

In terms of the number of races won, the Karl Burke-trained colt's second season was not as fruitful – he notched two wins and six unplaced finishes from eight starts – but he advertised himself to Irish mare owners and potential foal and yearling buyers by beating Caspian Prince by a length in the Group 2 Sapphire Stakes at the Curragh in July before returning there two months later to beat Son Of Rest by half a length in the newly promoted Group 1 Derrinstown Stud Flying Five Stakes. A patchy win-run record is not uncommon for sprinters, and this pale grey goes to stud as a Timeform 118-rated top-level winner.

He can also lay claim to being the fastest representative of the Galileo sire line, and he looks sure to prove popular in his new home at Whitsbury Manor Stud in Hampshire, the home of Group 1 sire and rising star Showcasing (by Oasis Dream). His initial fee has been set at £8,000.

Although one might be tempted to attribute his five-furlong speed to being out of a daughter of Dark Angel (by Acclamation), it should not be forgotten that the sire of a horse contributes half of the genetic make-up and his sire is out of the talented sprinter Jessica's Dream (by Desert Style) – a Group 3 Ballyogan Stakes winner who was third in the Group 2 Flying Five.

Havana Grey, who was bred by the partnership of Mickley Stud and Lady Lonsdale, made 42,000gns in Newmarket as a foal and €70,000 when reoffered as a yearling in Deauville. He is the first foal of five-furlong winner Blanc De Chine, and that half-sister to Group 3 Molecomb Stakes runner-up and triple sprint scorer Fast Act (by Fast Company) is a half-sister to the prolific duo Desert Opal (by Cadeaux Genereux) and Kuanyao (by American Post) – who won 28 races between them – and out of Nullarbor. This makes him inbred 4x3 to that mare's sire, Green Desert (by Danzig). No surprise then that sprinting was his game, and it will likely be the area in which many of his offspring also excel. He will also sire milers.

Nullarbor's half-brother Radevore (by Generous) won the Group 2 Prix Eugene Adam over 10 furlongs at Saint-Cloud and finished third to Helissio in the Group 2 Prix Niel over 12, and his dam's half-sister Peplum (by Nijinsky) won the Listed Cheshire Oaks before taking third to Always Friendly in the Group 3 Princess Royal Stakes at Ascot. It's no surprise, of course, for horses by their sires to prove effective over middle-distances, but there is plenty of mile and 10-furlong talent in the family too because the fourth dam of Havana Grey is Chain Store (by Nodouble), the stakes-winning dam of 1985's Group 1 Irish 1000 Guineas heroine Al Bahathri (by Blushing Groom).

She also won the Group 2 Coronation Stakes and Group 3 Child Stakes that year, she was the middle one in that memorable three-way photo-finish of short-heads in the Group 1 1000 Guineas at Newmarket, splitting Oh So Sharp and Bella Colora, and her record also included victory in the Group 2 Lowther Stakes as juvenile. She was the dam of Group 1 2000 Guineas and Group 1 Champion Stakes star Haafhd (by Alhaarth), and she lived in retirement at Derrinstown Stud until her death at the age of 32.

Al Bahathri was also the dam of seven-furlong Group 2 scorer Munir (by Indian Ridge), and grandam of eight and nine-furlong Group 1 star Gladiatorus (by Silic) and of Hong Kong's 10-furlong Group 1 standout Military Attack (by Oratorio). In stark contrast, her descendants also include Group 1 Gold Cup hero Big Orange (by Duke Of Marmalade) and Group 1 Hong Kong Vase scorer and triple Group 1 Melbourne Cup runner-up Red Cadeaux (by Cadeaux Genereux).

But that's not all you'll find on the page because Bloudan (by Damascus) – the third dam of Havana Grey – was also a half-sister to Chain Fern (by Blushing Groom), and that unraced filly achieved fame as the dam of ill-fated US Grade 1 star Spanish Fern (by El Gran Senor), grandam of Grade 1 Santa Anita Handicap scorer Heatseeker (by Giant's Causeway), and of one of last year's European classic stars. Chain Fern's unraced daughter Green Room (by Theatrical) is the mare who has given us Group 1 Prix Jean Prat winner and sire Lord Shanakill (by Speightstown), Group 1 Fillies' Mile scorer Together Forever (by Galileo), and 2018's Group 1 Investec Oaks heroine Forever Together (by Galileo).

Their relationship to Havana Grey is remote, even though they're by Galileo and share a direct ancestor in Chain Store, but their presence on the page does show some of the depth there is to this famous family. He is an interesting addition to the stallion ranks, and I look forward to seeing what he can do as a sire.

SUMMARY DETAILS

Standing: Whitsbury Manor Stud, Hampshire
Fee: £8,000

Career highlights: 6 wins inc Derrinstown Stud Flying Five Stakes (Gr1), Sapphire Stakes (Gr2), Bombay Sapphire Molecomb Stakes (Gr3), Allied World Dragon Stakes (L), Better Odds With Matchbook National Stakes (L), 2nd Darley Prix Morny (Gr1), Wainwrights Flying Childers Stakes (Gr2)
Other stallions by his sire include: none

HAVANA GREY (GB) – grey 2015

Havana Gold (IRE)	Teofilo (IRE)	Galileo (IRE)
		Speirbhean (IRE)
	Jessica's Dream (IRE)	Desert Style (IRE)
		Ziffany (GB)
Blanc De Chine (IRE)	Dark Angel (IRE)	Acclamation (GB)
		Midnight Angel (GB)
	Nullarbor (GB)	Green Desert (USA)
		Bloudan (USA)

HAWKBILL (USA)

The all-weather tracks have been a huge benefit to the racing industry in Britain, Ireland and France, and the number of Group 1 stars who got their maiden success on one of the artificial surfaces has been on the increase over the past few years.

Jack Hobbs, who was a three-length winner over eight and a half furlongs at Wolverhampton on his only juvenile start, chased home Golden Horn in the Derby at Epsom before taking the Irish Derby at the Curragh, and Covert Love, whose first start at three was a winning one at Chelmsford, went on to take the Irish Oaks at the Curragh, one of two Group 1 races the filly won that season. Classic and multiple Group 1 stars Seventh Heaven and Winter got their first wins at Dundalk (also the venue of Skitter Scatter's first win), Pretty Polly Stakes winner Nezwaah got off the mark at Chelmsford, Grand Prix de Saint-Cloud scorer Silverwave broke his maiden at Pornichet La Baule in France, mile Group 1 ace Zelzal won a maiden on Deauville's Polytrack, 2018's Melbourne Cup hero Cross Counter won both his first two starts at Wolverhampton, Lightning Spear won his maiden at Kempton, and even the mighty Enable began her career on an artificial surface, scoring on her debut at Newcastle, as did this year's Group 1 St James's Palace Stakes scorer Without Parole.

Hawkbill is another. He began his career with a forgettable effort over five furlongs at Newbury in mid-April of his juvenile season but showed some promise when third over seven furlongs on the Polytrack at Kempton two months later. Several weeks after that he narrowly won a maiden at Lingfield, and both his subsequent outings of 2015 were back at Kempton, an easy win in a seven-furlong nursery followed by a narrow defeat of subsequent listed scorer Steel Of Madrid in a four-runner contest over a mile.

Three all-weather wins from a total of five starts, with an official handicap rating of 98, was not a typical profile of a potential Group 1 star, but Hawkbill showed that he had improved over the winter when springing a 14/1 surprise in the Listed Newmarket Stakes over 10 furlongs, on turf, on his reappearance in late April of his three-year-old year. He then took another step up in grade and added the Group 3 Tercentenary Stakes over the same trip at Ascot. The ground was soft that day, as it was at Sandown when the white-faced chestnut extended his winning sequence to six with a half-length defeat of Group 1 Poule d'Essai des Poulains (French 2000 Guineas) winner The Gurkha in the Group 1 Coral-Eclipse, thereby becoming the first Group 1 winner in Europe for his sire, Kitten's Joy (by El Prado).

It was only a matter of time before that US champion sire achieved such a feat as the grandson of Sadler's Wells (by Northern Dancer) was not only a top turf horse himself, but he is arguably the premier source of turf horses in North America. His array of stars also includes Grade 1 Breeders' Cup Turf Sprint scorer Bobby's Kitten, who ran away with a listed sprint at Cork on his only start in Europe and is now a popular member of the stallion team at Lanwades Stud in Newmarket (first yearlings in 2019), and, of course, 2018's Cartier Horse of the Year, Roaring Lion, whose four Group 1 wins and Timeform rating of 130 made him a shining light in what was a very good year. He is now about to embark on a stallion career at Tweenhills Farm & Stud in Gloucestershire.

Hawkbill's best win at four was the Group 2 Princess of Wales's Stakes at Newmarket, in which he beat Frontiersman by three-parts of a length, and that came a month before he chased home Timeform 125-rated German star Dschingis Secret in the Group 1 Longines Grosser Preis von Berlin at Hoppegarten. Another month after that he was in action in Canada and failed by just a head to beat Johnny Bear the Grade 1 Northern Dancer Turf Stakes. Those three races are all over 12 furlongs, as are the two big ones he won at Meydan in March of 2018. First, he beat old rival Frontiersman by a head in the Group 2 Dubai City of Gold and then he trounced an admittedly not yet fully tuned-up Poet's Word by three lengths in the Group 1 Longines Dubai Sheema Classic.

When he returned to Europe, he finished third to Poet's Word and Cracksman in the Group 1 Prince of Wales's Stakes, eight lengths behind the latter, but three-parts of a length in front of the tragically ill-fated Derby-placed Group 2 scorer colt Cliffs Of Moher. He then went to Sandown for another crack at the Coral-Eclipse but had to settle for fourth while Roaring Lion and Saxon Warrior fought out a memorable finish. Cliffs Of Moher was third. He had one final run before his retirement was announced, but although sent off favourite and leading for the early part of the race, he finished down the field as Johnny Bear won a second edition of the Grade 1 Northern Dancer Turf Stakes, this time beating Mekhtaal by half a length.

His sire was bred by Kenneth and Sarah Ramsey and spent all his career at their Ramsey Farm until transferring to Hill 'N Dale Farms, also in Kentucky, where will soon start his second season. Of course, many in Europe will remember his sire, El Prado, who was trained by the great Vincent O'Brien and was one of the early Group 1 winners and juvenile stars for Sadler's Wells. He stood at Adena Springs in Kentucky and his total of 83 stakes-winning progeny also includes Grade 1 scorers such as Artie Schiller, Asi Siempre, Borrego, Paddy O'Prado, Spanish Moon and major US sire Medaglia d'Oro – the Jonabell Farm stallion who has given us Rachel Alexandra, Songbird, Talismanic, and many others of note.

As a Group 1-winning son of a champion sire who represents the Sadler's Wells sire line, Hawkbill will likely draw plenty of attention in his new role at Dalham Hall Stud in Newmarket, especially as he can also boast the attraction of coming from the immediate family of a champion sire whose Group/Grade 1-winning offspring include another winner of the Eclipse Stakes.

Hawkbill, one of three Kitten's Joy Grade 1 winners who are out of mares that represent the Storm Cat (by Storm Bird) sire line, was bred by the Helen K Groves Revokable Trust. The $350,000 graduate of the Keeneland September Yearling Sale was trained by Charlie Appleby, he is the second foal out of Trensa (by Giant's Causeway), and his younger half-brother,

Free Drop Billy (by Union Rags), is also about to begin a stallion career. He beat Bravazo by four lengths to take the Grade 1 Claiborne Breeders' Futurity over eight and a half furlongs on the dirt at Keeneland in 2017, and he is now a new member of the roster at Spendthrift Farm in Kentucky.

Trensa was a winner at three, four and five years of age and her multiple blacktype placings included the runners-up spot in a Grade 3 handicap at Del Mar. Her half-sister Batique (by Storm Cat) was also durable, notching up seven wins from two to six years of age, and that triple Grade 3-scorer's credentials also include setting a new course record over nine furlongs at Monmouth Park. Indeed, multiple successes, above-average form, and an ability to win at the age of four or older are frequently seen attributes in the family.

Tejida (by Rahy), who is out of Batique, won only four of her 23 starts, but she was Grade 3-placed over nine furlongs and a mile and a half as a five-year-old, and three times Grade 3-placed at the age of six.

The grandam of Hawkbill is Serape (by Fappiano), whom Helen Groves bred and raced, and the best of her five wins, from two to four years of age, came in the Grade 1 Ballerina Handicap over seven furlongs at Saratoga. Although her dam did not win at the highest level, she did beat Serape by win total and accumulated earnings. That mare, Mochila (by In Reality), was a nine-time scorer from two to four years of age, a Grade 1 Ruffian Handicap runner-up, and half-sister to the Grade 1 Breeders' Cup Mile hero and Eclipse Award winner Cozzene (by Caro).

He spent his stallion career at Gainesway Farm in Kentucky, was US champion sire in 1996 when his son Alphabet Soup won the Grade 1 Breeders' Cup Classic, and his other top-level winners include Mizzen Mast, Tikkanen, Star Of Cozzene, and the popular grey Environment Friend, whom Clive Brittain trained to win the Group 1 Coral-Eclipse Stakes in 1991. Coming from the immediate family of a champion sire boosts the prospects of both Hawkbill and Free Drop Billy doing well in their second careers.

Mochila, who was out of the unraced Ride The Trails (by Prince John), was also a half-sister to the Grade 2 Del Mar Oaks winner Movin' Money (by Dr Fager) and listed scorer Ivy Road (by Dr Fager), with the latter being the dam of the blacktype earners Addled (by Foolish Pleasure), Devil On Ice (by Devil's Bag) and Yurtu (by Fappiano), who won 23 races between them. Her three-time winning half-sister Mesabi (by Minnesota Mac) was the dam of the blacktype-placed eight-time winner Kunjar (by Fappiano), Wakonda (by Fappiano) – a dual blacktype scorer who got the bulk of her dozen wins from four to six years of age – and their full-sister Funistrada, who was Grade 1-placed at two, won the Grade 2 Fall Highweight Handicap at three, was a Grade 1-placed dual stakes winner at four and a listed race winner at five. The talented Conte Di Savoya (by Sovereign Dancer), who missed out on classic placing when fourth in the Kentucky Derby, and the Grade 2 La Prevoyante Handicap heroine Krisada (by Kris S) feature among Funistrada's progeny.

Hawkbill was an admirable and much-travelled horse who won 10 of his 24 starts, struck twice at the highest level, earned over £3.5 million in prize money, and earned Timeform ratings of 125, 123 and 123 at three, four and five years of age respectively. He is by a champion sire who represents the Sadler's Wells line, he is a half-brother to a mile Grade 1 winner in the US, and he comes from the family of a champion sire. All of this makes him an interesting new addition to the stallion ranks, and he looks like great value at an introductory fee of just £7,500. Some of his offspring may be more prominent as juveniles than he was – depending on the contribution of their dams – and his long-term potential would appear to be as a sire of milers and middle-distance horses.

SUMMARY DETAILS

Standing: Dalham Hall Stud, Newmarket
Fee: £7,500
Career highlights: 10 wins inc Longines Dubai Sheema Classic (Gr1), Coral-Eclipse (Gr1), Dubai City of Gold

sponsored by Emirates SkyCargo (Gr2), Al Rayyan Stakes
(Gr3), Tercentenary Stakes (Gr3), Havana Gold Newmarket
Stakes (L), 2nd Northern Dancer Turf Stakes (Gr1), 127th
Longines Grosser Preis von Berlin (Gr1), 3rd Prince of
Wales's Stakes (Gr1), Investec Coronation Cup (Gr1),
Pastorius Grosser Preis von Bayern (Gr1)
Other stallions by his sire include: Real Solution (winners),
Big Blue Kitten (yearlings), Bobby's Kitten (yearlings)

HAWKBILL (USA) – chestnut 2013

Kitten's Joy (USA)	El Prado (IRE)	Sadler's Wells (USA)
		Lady Capulet (USA)
	Kitten's First (USA)	Lear Fan (USA)
		That's My Hon (USA)
Trensa (USA)	Giant's Causeway (USA)	Storm Cat (USA)
		Mariah's Storm (USA)
	Serape (USA)	Fappiano (USA)
		Mochila (USA)

LANCASTER BOMBER (USA)

It's hard to believe that Lancaster Bomber won only twice in his 18-race career. He was multiple Group 1-placed at two and three years of age – Timeform-rated 113 and 122 respectively – and retired to the National Stud in Newmarket as the earner of over £1 million in prize money to go with a profile that was developed in four countries on two continents. Timeform raised him to 125 after his two-length defeat of ill-fated Derby-placed Group 2 scorer Cliffs Of Moher in the Group 1 Tattersalls Gold Cup at the Curragh in late May 2018, what proved to be his final start.

His dam Sun Shower (by Indian Ridge) was only placed, but his triple Group 3-winning half-brother Mull Of Killough (by Mull Of Kintyre), who was her first foal, won nine times in his career. This was one ahead of the final tally of his multiple Group 1-winning half-brother Excelebration (by Exceed And Excel), a Timeform 133-rated star who had the misfortune to run up against the great Frankel several times. Their dam had been exported to India after he was born and the second of her multiple winners out there was prolific blacktype scorer Shivalik Showers (by Dancing Forever), who has won a total of 14 times to date. However, Lancaster Bomber won just two. The mare moved to the US in 2012 and had full-brothers to her latest star in 2017 and 2018.

He chased home World Approval in both the Grade 1 Breeders' Cup Mile at Del Mar and the Grade 1 Ricoh Woodbine Mile Stakes in Canada, he was runner-up to his brother's star son Barney Roy in the Group 1 St James's Palace Stakes at Ascot and to Churchill in the Group 1 Dewhurst Stakes at Newmarket, fourth behind that same star in the Group 1 2000 Guineas, and third last year to Rhododendron and Lightning Spear in the Group 1 Juddmonte Lockinge Stakes at Newbury. It is an admirable record and one that fully entitles him to his place at stud.

Lancaster Bomber is one of 19 Group/Grade 1 winners by Claiborne Farm's outstanding stallion War Front (by Danzig), a horse who could forge the third branch of his sire's mighty line in the coming years. For so long it has been just his classic-placed, Group 1-winning sprinters Danehill and Green Desert who have made their dynasties – War Front was among his late representatives. It is too early in that potential development yet to make it better than perhaps a 66/1 shot, but the signs are promising as his early stallion sons include Declaration Of War (Olmedo) and The Factor (Noted And Quoted) who have one top-level winner apiece. Data Link has disappointed so far, War Command got a listed scorer among his high double-digit tally of first-crop winners in 2018, Air Force Blue's first crop arrived in 2018, Darley Japan-based American Patriot will have his first foals in 2019, and, like Lancaster Bomber, U S Navy Flag starts his stallion career in 2019.

Sun Shower was out of Miss Kemble (by Warning), a non-winning daughter of Group 1 Irish 1000 Guineas and Group 1 Yorkshire Oaks heroine Sarah Siddons (by Le Levanstell), and that made that mare a half-sister to record-breaking Group 1 Irish Oaks star Princess Pati (by Top Ville) and Group 2 Great Voltigeur Stakes winner Seymour Hicks (by Ballymore), the sire of Cheltenham Gold Cup and dual King George VI Chase star See More Business. Sarah Siddons was also responsible for dual stakes winner Sidara (by Golden Fleece) – grandam and third dam of Group 3-winning juvenile fillies Athlumney Lady (by Lycius) and Princess Iris (by Desert Prince) respectively – and of three others who went on to make their name at stud.

Dansara (by Dancing Brave) became the grandam of Group 2 Prix de Royallieu winner Sea Of Heartbreak (by Rock Of Gibraltar) and of Group 3 Ballysax Stakes scorer Puncher Clynch (by Azamour), whereas Princess Pati's full-sister Cantanta gave us Cantilever (by Sanglamore), the Group 2-placed, Group 3 Prix de Royaumont winner whose star grandson Wicklow Brave (by Beat Hollow) has won the Group 1 Irish St Leger. Then there's Gertrude Lawrence, a full-sister to Seymour Hicks but dam of the speedy stakes winner Lady Ambassador (by General Assembly). That one, in turn, became the dam of Group 1 Prix Vermeille heroine and

Group 1 Prix de l'Arc de Triomphe runner-up Leggera (by Sadler's Wells) and of Group 2-placed dual middle-distance pattern winner Lucido (by Royal Academy).

Stallions from the Danzig line have clicked well with Sun Shower, and the other Group 1 winner of 2018 out of an Indian Ridge mare was Irish 2000 Guineas scorer Romanised (by Holy Roman Emperor). She already has one son who has sired a Group 1 star and other stakes winners at stud, so it's no stretch of the imagination to think that she could do it again, with Lancaster Bomber. He looks likely to get his best juveniles over seven furlongs and a mile, and to get talented milers and middle-distance horses, and possibly some stayers, among his three-year-olds and older horses.

SUMMARY DETAILS

Standing: National Stud, Newmarket

Fee: £8,500

Career highlights: 2 wins inc Tattersalls Gold Cup (Gr1), 2nd Breeders' Cup Mile (Gr1), St James's Palace Stakes (Gr1), Ricoh Woodbine Mile Stakes (Gr1), Dubai Dewhurst Stakes (Gr1), Breeders' Cup Juvenile Turf (Gr1), 3rd Al Shaqab Lockinge Stakes (Gr1)

Other stallions by his sire include: Declaration Of War (Gr1), The Factor (Gr1), State Of Play (Gr2), Data Link (L), Soldat (L), War Command (L), Due Diligence (2yo of 2019), Jack Milton (2yo), Summer Front (2yo), Air Force Blue (yearlings), Hit It A Bomb (yearlings), War Correspondent (yearlings), War Dancer (yearlings), American Patriot (foals)

LANCASTER BOMBER (USA) – bay 2014

War Front (USA)	Danzig (USA)	Northern Dancer (CAN)
		Pas De Nom (USA)
	Starry Dreamer (USA)	Rubiano (USA)
		Lara's Star (USA)
Sun Shower (IRE)	Indian Ridge	Ahonoora
		Hillbrow
	Miss Kemble (GB)	Warning
		Sarah Siddons (FR)

LIGHTNING SPEAR (GB)

If at first you don't succeed, try, try, try again. It's an often-quoted motivational statement, but even the most enthusiastic could be forgiven for calling a halt when the number of misses reaches double digits. Lightning Spear's connections persevered, they got within a short-head of taking the Group 1 Juddmonte Lockinge Stakes at Newbury last year – pipped by Rhododendron – and just reward finally came at Goodwood on August 1st, the entire's 16th attempt at the highest level. He beat high-class three-year-old Expert Eye by one and a half lengths in the Qatar Sussex Stakes, with Lord Glitters another half-length back in third, a nose and neck ahead of Gustav Klimt and Beat The Bank.

The dual Group 2 Celebration Mile winner has six Group 1 placings to his name, including third to Accidental Agent in this year's Queen Anne Stakes at Ascot, but as he serves his first season on the stallion team at Tweenhills Farm & Stud, he is doing so as a Group 1-winning son of a leading international sire.

He was bred by Newsells Park Stud, and is a good-looking horse who made 260,000gns from Book 1 of the Tattersalls October Yearling Sal. He is by the sire of multiple Group 1-siring stallions Kyllachy (Sole Power, Twilight Son) and Siyouni (Ervedya, Laurens), and he comes from the family of a European champion sire – which makes him a likely candidate to get stakes and pattern-winning offspring at all levels, mostly in the six to 12-furlong range.

Lightning Spear was trained by Ralph Beckett when he won his only start as a juvenile, over seven furlongs on Polytrack at Kempton in August, making him yet another top-level scorer who got an early winning start on the artificial tracks (see the essay on Hawkbill). He was in the Olly Stevens stable when taking his only race at three, an eight-and-a-half-furlong contest at Nottingham. He won two more handicaps at four, lost his unbeaten record when chasing home Arod in the Group 2 Summer Mile at Ascot, and was fourth to

Esoterique in the Prix Jacques le Marois at Deauville a month later, his first Group 1 attempt.

Timeform rated him 125 as a five-year-old when he won his first Group 2 Celebration Mile – now trained by David Simcock – before taking third to Minding and Ribchester in the Group 1 Queen Elizabeth II Stakes, and that organisation had him on 124 for this year before his Goodwood success. The win saw him raised to 126, but then he put in three below-par performances. First, he was a two-and-a-half-length fifth to Recoletos in the Group 1 Prix du Moulin de Longchamp, then over seven lengths behind Roaring Lion when seventh in the Group 1 Queen Elizabeth II Stakes at Ascot, although he was beaten by less than three lengths when seventh to Expert Eye in the Grade 1 Breeders' Cup Mile at Churchill Downs.

The best of four blacktype earners out of multiple stakes-winning sprinter Atlantic Destiny (by Royal Academy), the half-brother to 10-furlong listed scorer Ocean War (by Dalakhani) is out of a half-sister to Make No Mistake (by Darshaan), who did well for the Dermot Weld stable. That talented colt carried the famous Moyglare Stud colours to victory in the Group 2 Royal Whip Stakes and Group 3 Meld Stakes at the Curragh, he was third in the Group 1 Tattersalls Gold Cup at the same venue and was also a Grade 2-placed dual Grade 3 winner in the USA.

Grandam Respectfully (by The Minstrel) was unplaced in a single start in France, and third dam Treat Me Nobly (by Vaguely Noble) – who made a record 1,300,000 francs as a yearling – was unraced, but the latter was out of What A Treat (by Tudor Minstrel), the US three-year-old filly champion of 1965, and so she was a half-sister to Be My Guest (by Northern Dancer). What A Treat, whose 11 wins included the Beldame Stakes, Alabama Stakes, and Gazelle Handicap, was out of the prolific Rare Treat (by Stymie) – which made her a half-sister to the dam of ill-fated Derby hero Golden Fleece (by Nijinsky) – and her star son was one of the early standout stallions for Coolmore Stud.

Be My Guest first came to prominence when setting a short-lived European record yearling price of 127,000gns when topping the Goffs Premier Yearling Sale in 1975. The Vincent O'Brien-trained, white-faced chestnut won the second of his two starts at two, kicked off his three-year-old campaign with an easy win in the Blue Riband Trial over eight and a half furlongs at Epsom, but was beaten twice when stepping up in trip – including in the Derby – before returning to a mile. He easily won the Desmond Stakes at the Curragh before, on soft ground at Goodwood, he fought to hold off the challenge of Don in the Waterford Crystal Mile. A bruised foot denied him the chance to run in the Queen Elizabeth II Stakes, and he went to stud as a Timeform 126-rated son of leading sire Northern Dancer (by Nearctic), whose growing list of significant winners included that year's Derby hero, The Minstrel.

Be My Guest was crowned European champion sire in 1982 when his first crop of three-year-olds featured Group 1 Prix du Jockey Club (French Derby), Group 1 Benson & Hedges Gold Cup (now Juddmonte International Stakes) and runaway Group 1 Irish Derby hero Assert, and star miler On The House, who took both the Group 1 1000 Guineas and Group 1 Sussex Stakes. His career roll of honour also featured Group 1 aces Double Bed, Go And Go, Luth Enchantee, Pelder, Pentire, and Valentine Waltz, and Group 2 Lockinge Stakes winner and Group 1 Derby runner-up Most Welcome, and although his sons met with mixed success at stud, many of his daughters excelled in that role.

If you go back farther on the page, then you find that the sixth dam of Lightning Spear was the speedy stakes winner Rare Perfume (by Eight Thirty). That made his fifth dam a half-sister to 1962's Belmont Stakes winner and US three-year-old champion Jaipur (by Nasrullah), whose progeny included dual Group 1 scorer and sprint champion Amber Rama, and Timeform 120-rated sprint juvenile Mansingh (sire of Petong).

Lightning Spear, the winner of seven of his 26 starts and over £1.3 million in prize money, has a pedigree that could see him do well as a sire and he is among the brightest new prospects who have joined the stallion ranks in 2019.

SUMMARY DETAILS

Standing: Tweenhills Farm & Stud, Gloucestershire
Fee: £8,500
Career highlights: 7 wins inc Qatar Sussex Stakes (Gr1), Celebration Mile (Gr2-twice), 2nd Al Shaqab Lockinge Stakes (Gr1-twice), Fred Cowley MBE Memorial Summer Mile (Gr2), 3rd Queen Anne Stakes (Gr1-twice), Qatar Sussex Stakes (Gr1), Queen Elizabeth II Stakes (Gr1), Clipper Logistics Boomerang Stakes (Gr2)
Other stallions by his sire include: Captain Rio (Gr1), Excellent Art (Gr1), Falco (Gr1), Kyllachy (Gr1), Siyouni (Gr1), Farhh (Gr2), Windsor Knot (Gr3), Needwood Blade (winners), Nephrite (winners), Noordhoek Flyer, Virtual (winners), Eagle Top (yearlings)

LIGHTNING SPEAR (GB) – chestnut 2011

Pivotal (GB)	Polar Falcon (USA)	Nureyev (USA)
		Marie D'Argonne (FR)
	Fearless Revival	Cozzene (USA)
		Stufida
Atlantic Destiny (IRE)	Royal Academy (USA)	Nijinsky (CAN)
		Crimson Saint (USA)
	Respectfully (USA)	The Minstrel (CAN)
		Treat Me Nobly (USA)

MASSAAT (IRE)

Massaat was seen in action just three times in each of his three seasons to race, but those glimpses showed him to be a high-class performer who likely had the ability to succeed at the highest level. His only pattern win was a one-and-three-quarter-length defeat of Librisa Breeze in the Group 2 Betfred Hungerford Stakes over seven furlongs at Newbury as a four-year-old, but he had chased home Air Force Blue in the Dewhurst as a juvenile, and Galileo Gold in the 2000 Guineas at three, and he was certainly not disgraced when chasing home Ribchester and Taareef in the Group 1 Qatar Prix du Moulin de Longchamp on his penultimate start. Timeform rated him 114p at two, 122 at three, and 121 at four.

The Owen Burrows-trained bay, whose final run was when chasing home Limato in the Group 2 Godolphin Challenge Stakes at Newmarket in October 2017, is among the early sons of leading international sire Teofilo (by Galileo) to go to stud, and it will be fascinating to see how his career turns out. The first of the sons to have any runners is Tweenhills Farm & Stud's mile Group 1 star Havana Gold whose first crop features Group 1-winning sprinter and 2019 new sire Havana Grey. That augurs well for those who are in earlier stages of their career.

Massaat comes from a prolific blacktype family that got a significant boost in both 2017 and 2018, and the latter was the Group 1 Commonwealth Cup victory of his half-brother Eqtidaar (by Invincible Spirit). Hopefully that Sir Michael Stoute-trained colt can enhance his record further this year. The other big update appears under the second generation of the pedigree. Madany (by Acclamation), his winning dam, is a half-sister to the pattern-winning sprinter Dolled Up (by Whipper) and to multiple listed scorer Zeiting (by Zieten), and the latter is a prolific blacktype producer at stud. She is the dam of Group 2-winning miler Combat Zone (by Refuse To Bend), of middle-distance Group 3 scorer Royal Empire (by Teofilo), and of Group 3 Strensall Stakes winner and Group 1

Caulfield Cup runner-up Scottish (by Teofilo), plus three stakes-placed daughters. One of the three is Group 3-placed Zut Alors (by Pivotal), and she is the dam of 2017's Group 1 Poule d'Essai des Pouliches (French 1000 Guineas) star Precieuse (by Tamayuz).

Belle De Cadix (by Law Society), the winning grandam of Massaat, is a half-sister to a trio of top-class performers in India, and her unraced dam Gourgandine (by Auction Ring) was a daughter of Group 2 Ribblesdale Stakes runner-up North Forland (by Northfields). That made her a half-sister to Group 1-placed Group 2 Prix d'Harcourt winner Fortunes Wheel (by Law Society), to Group 1 Poule d'Essai des Pouliches third and Italian Group 2 scorer Libertine (by Hello Gorgeous), and to Harmless Albatross (by Pas De Seul), a Group 1-placed pattern winner as a juvenile. Libertine is also notable as being the grandam of Group 2 Lowther Stakes winner Infamous Angel (by Exceed And Excel), whereas Harmless Albatross came up with middle-distance listed winners Ghataas (by Sadler's Wells) and Kahtan (by Nashwan) as well as Group 1-placed US Grade 2 scorer and blacktype sire Volochine (by Soviet Star).

With two Group 1 winners added to the page in the past two years, this is a pedigree that is gaining strength, and there could be more updates of note by the time Massaat's first offspring reach the sales ring. He should be capable of getting winners in all age groups, with most proving effective in the five to 10-furlong range.

SUMMARY DETAILS

Standing: Mickley Stud, Shropshire
Fee: £5,000
Career highlights: 2 wins inc Betfred Hungerford Stakes (Gr2), 2nd Qipco 2000 Guineas (Gr1), Dubai Dewhurst Stakes (Gr1), Godolphin Challenge Stakes (Gr2), 3rd Prix du Moulin de Longchamp (Gr1)
Other stallions by his sire include: Havana Gold (Gr1), Amira's Prince (2yo in 2019), Kermadec (2yo in 19/20), Parish Hall (yearlings), Portage (foals)

MASSAAT (IRE) – bay 2013

Teofilo (IRE)	Galileo (IRE)	Sadler's Wells (USA)
		Urban Sea (USA)
	Speirbhean (IRE)	Danehill (USA)
		Saviour (USA)
Madany (IRE)	Acclamation (GB)	Royal Applause (GB)
		Princess Athena
	Belle De Cadix (IRE)	Law Society (USA)
		Gourgandine

MASTER CARPENTER (IRE)

Do you want to breed your mare to a new stallion who represents a major male line and comes from a proven sire-producing family? How about one who showed talent at two and can boast relationship to Invincible Spirit and Kodiac? If that's what you are looking for, then you have three horses to choose from in 2019. Classic-placed juvenile Group 2 scorer Gustav Klimt and Group 1-placed juvenile Group 2 scorer James Garfield are in Ireland, but Master Carpenter (by Mastercraftsman) is in England, near Newmarket.

He spent much of his career running over eight to 10 and a half furlongs, getting his final win when defying top-weight in a nine-furlong handicap at Goodwood in September, but look at his juvenile record, and you will find that he made a winning debut over five furlongs at Leicester in early April of that year, scoring by two and a half lengths. He was then third in a five-furlong conditions race at Ascot, won easily over six furlongs at Pontefract, and was among the market leaders for the Listed Chesham Stakes over seven furlongs at Royal Ascot.

He was unplaced that day, made the frame in a pair of nurseries in the autumn, and finished third to Kingman in the Group 3 Greenham Stakes on his seasonal reappearance at three. He filled the same position behind Western Hymn in the Group 3 Classic Trial at Sandown later that month, was runner-up in the Listed Fairway Stakes over 10 furlongs at Newmarket in mid-May, and then ran away with a one-mile listed contest at Sandown, scoring by seven lengths. A month later, he beat Calling Out by half a length to take the Group 3 Prix Daphnis over nine furlongs at Chantilly, three weeks before taking third to old rival Western Hymn in the Group 2 Prix Eugene Adam over 10 at Maisons-Laffitte. He won the prestigious John Smith's Cup (heritage handicap) at York as a four-year-old, shortly before taking the runners-up spot in the Group 3 Rose of Lancaster Stakes at Haydock, and added two more blacktype placings to his name at the age of five.

Master Carpenter is the best of several winners out of Fringe (by In The Wings), a mare who was never worse than fourth in an eight-race career and whose sole win was a five-length score over 10 furlongs at Goodwood as a four-year-old. She could be described as being a three-parts-sister to Mount Elbrus (by Barathea), who beat Shamdara by a length in a 10-and-a-half-furlong listed contest on heavy ground at Saint-Cloud before being a blacktype producer at stud. Her daughter Lava Flow (by Dalakhani) won an 11-furlong listed contest in France, and her lightly raced son Strobilus (by Mark Of Esteem) was short-headed by Kirklees in the Group 1 Gran Criterium over a mile at San Siro on his final run as a juvenile.

They are out of El Jazirah (by Kris), which means that Master Carpenter's grandam is a full-sister to Group 1 Prix de Diane (French Oaks) heroine Rafha, the dam of significant sires Invincible Spirit (by Green Desert) and Kodiac (by Danehill). Also of note are that Rafha's half-sister Chiang Mai (by Sadler's Wells) is the Group 3 Blandford Stakes-winning dam of Group 1 Pretty Polly Stakes heroine Chinese White (by Dalakhani), that half-sister Wosaita (by Generous) is the grandam of the aforementioned James Garfield (by Exceed And Excel), that half-sister Al Anood (by Danehill) is the stakes-placed dam of dual Australian juvenile Group 1 star and reverse-shuttle stallion Pride Of Dubai (by Street Cry), and that Kodiac's stakes-winning full-sister Massarra is the dam of both juvenile mile Group 1 scorer Nayarra (by Cape Cross) and the aforementioned Gustav Klimt (by Galileo).

There are many more stakes and pattern winners in this famous family, and you will find classic sire Pitcairn (by Petingo) and Group 1 stayer star Assessor (by Niniski) under the fourth dam, but they tell us nothing more than we already know about Master Carpenter's stallion potential. He is slightly more closely related to Kodiac than he is to Invincible Spirit, but both of those star stallions are out of a full-sister to his grandam. This, combined with his April juvenile maiden success, his pattern-winning and plenty of blacktype form, and being a representative of the Danehill sire line, makes him an intriguing addition to the stallion ranks.

SUMMARY DETAILS
Standing: GG Bloodstock and Racing, Kirtling
Fee: £2,000
Career highlights: 7 wins inc Prix Daphnis (Gr3), Cantor Fitzgerald Corporate Finance Heron Stakes (L), 2nd Betfred Rose of Lancaster Stakes (Gr3), Tamdown Fairway Stakes (L), 3rd Prix Eugene Adam (Gr2), Betway Huxley Stakes (Gr3), Aon Greenham Stakes (Gr3), bet365 Classic Trial (Gr3), Sky Bet Go-Racing-In-Yorkshire Summer Festival Pomfret Stakes (L)
Other stallions by his sire include: Kingston Hill (2yo in 2019), The Grey Gatsby (foals)

MASTER CARPENTER (IRE) – chestnut 2011

Mastercraftsman (IRE)	Danehill Dancer (IRE)	Danehill (USA)
		Mira Adonde (USA)
	Starlight Dreams (USA)	Black Tie Affair
		Reves Celestes (USA)
Fringe (GB)	In The Wings	Sadler's Wells (USA)
		High Hawk
	El Jazirah (GB)	Kris
		Eljazzi

POET'S WORD (IRE)

A surprising number of stallions died in the first few months of 2018 and although some of them were, as one might expect, elderly horses living in retirement, several were much younger. The latter include Group 1-winning miler and Dalham Hall Stud resident Poet's Voice, one of the early sire sons of Dubawi (by Dubai Millennium). His initial foals and yearlings lit up the auction ring, his eldest offspring are now six years old, he shuttled to Australia, and he has accumulated a double-digit tally of stakes winners.

However, before the start of 2018, he had no Group 1 winner to his name and the best of blacktype scorers included Group 2 Mehl-Mulhens Rennen (German 2000 Guineas) winner Poetic Dream and Italian Group 3 mile classic scorers Mi Raccomando (Premio Regina Elena) and Poeta Diletto (Premio Parioli). His southern hemisphere stint had yielded the Group 1-placed Group 2 Roman Consul Stakes winner Viridine – who is out of an Anabaa (by Danzig) mare – three listed race scorers, and also Group 1 Australian Oaks runner-up Perfect Rhyme, who is out of a daughter of Danehill (by Danzig).

For a horse of whom so much was expected, this was a disappointing overall record, but there was one among the 13 whose 2017 form suggested he could go on to strike at the highest level. Of course, it is all but guaranteed that there are more stakes and pattern winners still to emerge from his younger offspring, some of whom could become racehorses of real note, so the story of Poet's Voice certainly did not end with his premature death. Indeed, in 2018 his blacktype tally included Australian Group 1 winner Trap For Fools, Group 2 Derby Italiano scorer Summer Festival, Group 2 Oaks d'Italia heroine Sand Zabeel, and juvenile Group 3 winner Arctic Sound.

Poet's Word was that promising son from 2017, and he did indeed fulfil his potential by hitting the very top in 2018. The Sir Michael Stoute-trained bay represents his late sire's first crop, and he is now a member of the stallion team at Nunnery Stud in Norfolk. The new recruit excelled as a middle-distance horse, but that does not mean that he will be a source of only similar types at stud, as he's the son of a miler and from the family of a speedy horse who went on to sire several Group 1 stars from six to 10 and a half furlongs, including a classic winner, despite dying at a young age.

Poet's Word was bred by Woodcote Stud, was fourth over seven furlongs on his only start at two, won handicaps over 10 and 11 furlongs at Nottingham and Goodwood from five starts at three, and was among the leading older horses in Europe at the age of four. He began that campaign with handicap success at Chelmsford, was only beaten a neck by Deauville in the Group 3 Huxley Stakes over the extended 10 furlongs at Chester and then landed the Group 3 Betfred Glorious Stakes over 12 on soft ground at Goodwood, beating Second Step by a length and a half. That was a useful effort, but it is what he did after in the latter part of that season that was impressive, even though those three runs all ended in defeat.

First, he failed by just half a length to beat Decorated Knight in the Group 1 Qipco Irish Champion Stakes at Leopardstown, he chased home Cracksman in the Group 1 Qipco Champion Stakes at Ascot, was only beaten about five lengths when sixth to Time Warp in the Group 1 Longines Hong Kong Cup at Sha Tin. Timeform rated him 124. His sire received a figure of 126 from that same organisation, but the son now has the father beaten as he retired to stud having earned a Timeform mark of 132 after his pair of Group 1 victories.

Poet's Word kicked off his 2018 campaign by chasing home Hawkbill in the Group 1 Longines Dubai Sheema Classic at Meydan in late March, was an odds-on winner of the Group 3 Matchbook Brigadier Gerard Stakes over 10 furlongs at Sandown two months later, and then caused something of a sensation when taking the Group 1 Prince of Wales's Stakes over the same trip at Royal Ascot in June, beating the brilliant

Cracksman by two and a quarter lengths and with old rival Hawkbill another eight lengths back in third.

It was an excellent performance, even allowing for the fact that Cracksman did not run up to his best (and had reportedly sustained a head injury coming out of the stalls). The third, also now retired, is a good horse and proven multiple Group 1 star whose wins include the Coral-Eclipse Stakes over that trip. A month later, over a quarter-mile farther at the same venue, Poet's Word proved that his newfound level of talent was no one-off performance as he beat Crystal Ocean by a neck to take the Group 1 King George VI and Queen Elizabeth Stakes, also on fast ground. This time the additional margin back to the third was nine lengths, with the spot filled by the high-class filly Coronet.

After this, it was on to York for the Group 1 Juddmonte International Stakes over 10-and-a-quarter furlongs, and he was sent off favourite to complete a top-level hat-trick. This day, however, he had to settle for the runners-up spot as Roaring Lion, who had won the Coral-Eclipse on his previous start, powered to victory by three and a quarter lengths. Thundering Blue, the only non-Group 1 winner in the line-up, ran a huge race to be third, with 2000 Guineas hero and Eclipse runner-up Saxon Warrior fourth.

A rematch with Roaring Lion – now finally showing the full potential he had promised – was eagerly anticipated, but while that colt went on to add the Group 1 Qipco Irish Champion Stakes and Group 1 Queen Elizabeth II Stakes en route to a new stallion career at Tweenhills Farm and Stud in Gloucestershire, Poet's Word did not make it back to the track. He had been among the ante-post favourites for the Group 1 Qipco Champion Stakes and Grade 1 Breeders' Cup Turf at Churchill Downs but sustained an injury shortly after York. His retirement was announced in mid-September.

The first point of note about the distaff side of his pedigree is that he is the sixth foal of Whirly Bird (by Nashwan), and that makes him a half-brother to two fillies of note: the talented former Mick Channon-trainee Malabar (by Raven's Pass) and two-time scorer Whirly Dancer (by Danehill

Dancer). The latter is the dam of last year's Group 2 Railway Stakes winner Beckford (by Bated Breath), who was runner-up in the Group 1 National Stakes and Group 1 Phoenix Stakes for the Gordon Elliott stable before moving to the USA, where he has won a five-furlong turf listed race for trainer Brendan Walsh, on his only start to date.

Malabar, on the other hand, won the Group 3 Prestige Stakes over seven furlongs at two, added the Group 3 Thoroughbred Stakes over a mile at three – both at Goodwood – and although the performances do not count for blacktype, she was fourth in each of the Group 1 1000 Guineas, Group 1 Prix Marcel Boussac and Group 1 Moyglare Stud Stakes.

Their dam was trained by Amanda Perrett, won five of her seven starts, and earned her blacktype when finishing third in the Listed Harvest Stakes over 11 and a half furlongs at Windsor on her final outing, so it is no surprise that Poet's Word stayed middle-distances. Her half-brother Ursa Major (by Galileo) won a 14-furlong Group 3 contest at the Curragh a month before finishing fourth to Encke, Camelot, and Michelangelo in the Group 1 St Leger at Doncaster, and the pair also have two half-sisters of note.

Inchiri (by Sadler's Wells) won a listed contest over 12 furlongs, and Inchberry (by Barathea) was a maiden in eight starts but listed-placed over a mile at Pontefract and missed out on a more notable accolade – classic placing – when finishing a two and a half-length fourth to Casual Look in the Group 1 Oaks at Epsom. She is also the dam of Measuring Time (by Dubai Destination) who was placed in several middle-distance pattern events.

They are all out of one-time scorer Inchyre (by Shirley Heights), and so the third dam of Poet's Word is Inchmurrin (by Lomond). A stakes-winning sprinter at two, she went on to beat classic-placed Dabaweyaa by five lengths in the Group 2 Child Stakes (now Falmouth Stakes) at Newmarket, shortly after chasing home Magic Of Life in the Group 1 Coronation Stakes at Ascot, and her final start resulted in a fourth-place finish to Sudden Love in the Grade 1 E P Taylor Stakes at

Woodbine. The best of her offspring was the Group 1-placed triple Group 3 scorer Inchinor (by Ahonoora) – who died at the age of 13 – and so Poet's Word's grandam is a half-sister to the sire of Group 1 stars Cape Of Good Hope, Latice, Notnowcato, Silca's Sister and Summoner.

Inchinor's stakes-winning half-sister Ingozi (by Warning) is the dam of Grade 1 E P Taylor Stakes heroine Miss Keller (by Montjeu) and grandam of Group 1 St Leger star Harbour Law (by Lawman). The long list of stakes and pattern winners among Inchmurrin's descendants also include Agent Murphy (by Cape Cross), Ayaar (by Rock Of Gibraltar), Blue Bayou (by Bahamian Bounty), Fantastic Pick (by Fantastic Light), Hatta Fort (by Cape Cross), and Venus De Milo (by Duke Of Marmalade). This selection represents a mixture of speed and stamina.

If you go back another step and take a look at the record of the fourth dam On Show (by Welsh Pageant) then you find that Inchmurrin was a half-sister to Group 2 Mill Reef Stakes winner Welney (by Habitat) and full-sister to Balnaha, the winning dam of Group 1 Coronation Stakes scorer Balisada (by Kris). However, it is Poet's Word's relationship to Inchinor that is most eye-catching when it comes to considering his prospects as a stallion.

Stud success sometimes skips a generation in mares – so, given his relationship to Inchinor, might we see this in Poet's Word? Seeking The Gold (by Mr Prospector) was an excellent stallion, but his brilliant son Dubai Millennium got just five stakes winners from his sole crop. One of the five was Group 1 winner and outstanding sire Dubawi, whose son Poet's Voice has done okay without qualifying for the label 'a good sire', but has among his 16 stakes winners a top-class son who has joined the team at a famous stud farm. Time will tell.

SUMMARY DETAILS
Standing: Nunnery Stud, Norfolk
Fee: £7,000
Career highlights: 7 wins inc King George VI and Queen Elizabeth Stakes (sponsored by Qipco) (Gr1), Prince of

Wales's Stakes (Gr1), Matchbook Brigadier Gerard Stakes
(Gr3), Betfred Glorious Stakes (Gr3), 2nd Juddmonte
International Stakes (Gr1), Longines Dubai Sheema Classic
(Gr1), Qipco Irish Champion Stakes (Gr1), Qipco Champion
Stakes (Gr1), sportingbet.com Huxley Stakes (Gr3)
Other stallions by his sire include: none

POET'S WORD (IRE) – bay 2013

Poet's Voice (GB)	Dubawi (IRE)	Dubai Millennium (GB)
		Zomaradah (GB)
	Bright Tiara (USA)	Chief's Crown (USA)
		Expressive Dance (USA)
Whirly Bird (GB)	Nashwan (USA)	Blushing Groom (FR)
		Height Of Fashion (FR)
	Inchyre (GB)	Shirley Heights
		Inchmurrin (IRE)

RAJASINGHE (IRE)

Many breeders prize early two-year-old speed, and that is what Rajasinghe possessed. He was a four-length winner over six furlongs on the Tapeta at Newcastle on his debut in mid-May, won the Group 2 Coventry Stakes by a head at Royal Ascot in June, and then finished third to Cardsharp in the Group 2 Arqana July Stakes at Newmarket. These efforts are in contrast to his only other starts, in which he was well-beaten in the Group 1 Juddmonte Middle Park Stakes, Grade 1 Breeders' Cup Juvenile Turf, and Group 1 Qipco 2000 Guineas, and both his official handicap mark and his Timeform rating at the end of his two-year-old season stood at 107.

He is a son of top sprinter Choisir (by Danehill Dancer) – who stayed a mile, and reverse-shuttled for several years – and that stallion's handful of early sire sons include Starspangledbanner (sire of Group 1 scorer The Wow Signal), Stimulation (sire of Group 3 winner Sweet Selection), and Olympic Glory, who was a blacktype sire in 2018 with his first juveniles. They also include the popular Group 1 Middle Park Stakes winner The Last Lion whose first foals made up to 60,000gns in 2018.

Rajasinghe's half-sister Kurland (by Kheleyf) was also an easy winner on her juvenile debut, taking a five-furlong contest at Newmarket in mid-April, and although she missed out on blacktype when finishing fourth to Acapulco in the Group 2 Queen Mary Stakes at Royal Ascot, she picked some up when third in a five-furlong listed contest at York two months later. Their half-sister Star Fire (by Dark Angel) has won four sprints in England, none as a two-year-old, and their dam is the precocious Bunditten (by Soviet Star) who made a winning debut in March of her juvenile year and was third in the Listed National Stakes before finishing fourth (no blacktype) to Damson in the Group 2 Queen Mary Stakes.

His grandam is Felicita (by Catrail), who was a pattern-placed dual listed sprint winner in France at two, her stakes-placed half-sister Anemone Garden (by Dancing Dissident) is the grandam of Group 1-placed multiple Australian five-and-a-half-furlong Group 2 scorer Super Cash (by Written Tycoon), and his fourth dam is 1968's 1000 Guineas heroine Caergwrle (by Crepello).

It remains to be seen what sort of support Rajasinghe will attract and what physical characteristics he passes on, but he is a horse who is bred for speed and precocity and showed those traits on the track. Some of his offspring may show talent at a mile, but it seems likely that most will be sprinters.

SUMMARY DETAILS

Standing: National Stud, Newmarket
Fee: £5,000
Career highlights: 2 wins inc Coventry Stakes (Gr2), 3rd Arqana July Stakes (Gr2)
Other stallions by his sire include: Starspangledbanner (Gr1), Stimulation (Gr3), Olympic Glory (L), Choistar (winners), The Last Lion (yearlings in 2019), Divine Prophet (foals)

RAJASINGHE (IRE) – bay 2015

Choisir (AUS)	Danehill Dancer (IRE)	Danehill (USA)
		Mira Adonde (USA)
	Great Selection (AUS)	Lunchtime
		Pensive Mood (AUS)
Bunditten (IRE)	Soviet Star (USA)	Nureyev (USA)
		Veruschka (FR)
	Felicita (IRE)	Catrail (USA)
		Abergwrle

ROARING LION (USA)

The phenomenal legacy left by triple Group 1 star and prolific champion sire Sadler's Wells (by Northern Dancer) has been felt around the world. In Europe, many will immediately identify his sons Galileo and Montjeu as having forged powerful branches of his line, with some of us who have been around for a while also naming In The Wings – the first of the significant Sadler's Wells sire sons here – as having had an influence too.

In North America, however, it is the former Vincent O'Brien-trained Group 1 National Stakes winner El Prado who achieved lasting fame. The grey came from the fourth crop of Sadler's Wells, he stood at Adena Springs in Kentucky, his 83 stakes winners included eight who won at the highest level, and two of his Grade 1-winning sons have become titans: Medaglia d'Oro and Kitten's Joy. The latter, a Ramsey Farm homebred who was a Grade 1 winner over 10 and 12 furlongs on turf, and commanded a fee of $100,000 from 2014 to 2017. He moved to Hill 'N Dale Farms in Kentucky in 2018, covering for $60,000, and is available there for $75,000 in 2019.

His is not a profile of a horse who would have been expected to make such an impact on that side of the Atlantic, and yet this champion sire has achieved progeny earnings in excess of $10 million every year from 2013 to 2018 and gets a high number of individual stakes winners each season. His progeny earned more than $18.6 million worldwide in 2018, placing him ahead of Candy Ride ($17.9 million), the late Scat Daddy ($15.7 million), and Mendelssohn's half-brother Into Mischief ($13.8 million) among US stallions. More than $10 million of his total was earned in North America alone, which was the ninth highest such figure of the year.

His Grade 1 Breeders' Cup Turf Sprint winner Bobby's Kitten – who was a runaway winner of a listed sprint at Cork on his only start in Ireland, and had his first foals in 2018 – stands at Lanwades Stud in Newmarket, and he has two

Group 1-winning sons and a Group 2 scorer joining the European stallion ranks in 2019. The latter is the high-class miler Taareef, who will stand at Haras Du Mezeray in France, and the other two are Hawkbill and Roaring Lion.

Hawkbill added 2018's Group 1 Dubai Sheema Classic at Meydan, in which he beat Poet's Word by three lengths, to his half-length defeat of The Gurkha in the Group 1 Coral-Eclipse at Sandown in 2016. Godolphin's widely travelled chestnut was trained by Charlie Appleby, he bowed out with a record of 10 wins from 24 starts and over £3.5 million in prize money and has joined the team at Dalham Hall Stud.

Qatar Racing Ltd's Roaring Lion, however, is best of all of their sire's European runners, and quite possibly his best anywhere in the world. The Timeform 130-rated grey, who was crowned Cartier Horse of the Year, has retired to Tweenhills Farm & Stud in Gloucestershire as a four-time Group 1 star whose eight wins from 13 starts yielded over £2.7 million in earnings. He looks sure to be very popular in his new role.

The John Gosden-trained colt made a winning debut over a mile at Newmarket's July course in mid-August of his juvenile season, followed that with a six-length score over the same trip on the Polytrack at Kempton, and then gamely beat Nelson by a neck in the Group 2 Juddmonte Royal Lodge Stakes. A month later, he looked set for victory in the Group 1 Racing Post Trophy at Doncaster before veering off a straight course and then losing out by a neck to Saxon Warrior.

The pair met again in the Group 1 Qipco 2000 Guineas at Newmarket in early May, which Saxon Warrior won by a length and a half and a head from Tip Two Win and Masar, with Roaring Lion another three-parts of a length back in fifth. Of course, both he and Masar improved considerably after that. The Masar who won the Group 1 Investec Derby at Epsom was more like the Masar who ran away with the Group 3 bet365 Craven Stakes at Newmarket – where Roaring Lion finished a rusty third – whereas the grey's impressive Group 2 Betfred Dante Stakes victory at York and his Derby third –

where Saxon Warrior was fourth – were just a hint of what was to come.

Roaring Lion and Saxon Warrior renewed their rivalry at Sandown a month after Epsom, and this time the grey won the battle, by a neck from the bay, taking their score to two apiece. The pair pulled two and a half lengths clear of third-placed Cliffs Of Moher who was, in turn, a length and a quarter in front of Hawkbill.

Round five was eagerly anticipated, and it came about in the Group 1 Juddmonte International Stakes at York. Dual Group 1 star Poet's Word was sent off favourite ahead of Roaring Lion and Saxon Warrior, the line-up was completed by Group 1 winners Benbatl, Latrobe, Thunder Snow and Without Parole and the improving Group 2 scorer Thundering Blue, making it the toughest test yet for the three-year-old rivals. It was arguably the brightest moment of Roaring Lion's career as powered to a three-and-a-quarter-length victory from the favourite, with Thundering Blue running a huge race in third, a length and a quarter ahead of Saxon Warrior.

Three-two became four-two when the colts met for the sixth and final time, in the Group 1 Qipco Irish Champion Stakes over 10 furlongs at Leopardstown. Saxon Warrior went to the front under a quarter of a mile from home and briefly looked like he might hold on as Roaring Lion began his challenge, but the grey got there to win by a neck. It soon emerged that the runner-up had sustained an injury and would be retired immediately, which was unfortunate. That colt is now on the Coolmore roster for 2019.

Although a proven star over 10 furlongs, Roaring Lion's connections decided to bypass the Group 1 Qipco Champion Stakes in favour of the one-mile Group 1 Queen Elizabeth Stakes on the same card, at the Qipco British Champions Day at Ascot in October. It was the right call as there was no horse in Europe – possibly in the world – who could have beaten Cracksman that day as the Timeform 136-rated champion ran away with the race for the second consecutive year.

The bare form of beating I Can Fly by a neck, with Century Dream a half-length back in third and another three-parts of a length to Stormy Antarctic, is some way below the heights he achieved in his other top-level wins, but Roaring Lion stayed on gamely to land the spoils and complete his Group 1 four-timer over a trip just short of his best distance. His final outing, when never a factor in the Grade 1 Breeders' Cup Classic on dirt at Churchill Downs, can be ignored. He's not a dirt horse – which is typical for offspring of Kitten's Joy – and it takes nothing away from his exceptional talent on turf.

Roaring Lion was bred by Ranjan Racing Inc, he is a $160,000 graduate of the Keeneland September Yearling Sale, and he is related to a string of high-class performers, most of whom did well at around a mile. The first foal of Vionnet (by Street Sense), who was a three-quarter-length third in the 10-furlong Grade 1 Rodeo Drive Stakes on turf at Santa Anita, he is a grandson of the prolific Cambiocorsa (by Avenue Of Flags), a dual Grade 3 scorer over six and a half furlongs on the downhill turf course at that same venue.

That mare, who won nine of her 18 starts, has excelled at stud, coming up with five blacktype offspring from six runners, and in addition to Vionnet, they are nine-furlong Grade 2 winner Moulin De Mougin (by Curlin), Grade 2-winning miler Schiaparelli (by Ghostzapper), and mile listed scorers Alexis Tangier (by Tiznow) and Bronson (by Medaglia d'Oro) – all turf horses. Cambiocorsa also has the distinction of being a full-sister to the high-class sprinter California Flag, whose double-digit tally included three editions of the six-and-a-half-furlong Grade 3 Morvich Handicap at Santa Anita.

They, in turn, are out of Ultrafleet (by Afleet), who failed to make the frame in four attempts, and that daughter of multiple stakes-placed six-time winner Social Conduct (by Vigors) is a half-sister to Social Service (by Green Forest), the five-time winning dam of multiple stakes-winning filly Princess Deelite (by Afternoon Deelites).

All of this pointed to Roaring Lion as being a potentially high-class mile-to-10-furlong horse who, depending on the amount of stamina he had received from his sire, could stay the Derby distance – and that's how he turned out. It also makes him a fascinating new addition to the stallion ranks. He represents a cross of the El Prado branch of the Sadler's Wells (by Northern Dancer) line with the Machiavellian branch of the Mr Prospector (by Raise a Native) line, he never ran over less than a mile, and he went from being a Timeform 120p-rated juvenile to a four-time Group 1 star rated 130. His two-year-olds will likely be seen to best effect over seven furlongs and upwards, and his best offspring are likely to do well anywhere in the broad seven-to-14-furlong range.

SUMMARY DETAILS

Standing: Tweenhills Farm & Stud, Gloucestershire
Fee: £40,000
Career highlights: 8 wins inc Queen Elizabeth II Stakes (Gr1), Qipco Irish Champion Stakes (Gr1), Juddmonte International Stakes (Gr1), Coral-Eclipse Stakes (Gr1), Betfred Dante Stakes (Gr2), Juddmonte Royal Lodge Stakes (Gr2), 2nd Racing Post Trophy (Gr1), 3rd Investec Derby (Gr1)
Other stallions by his sire include: Real Solution (winners), Big Blue Kitten (yearlings), Bobby's Kitten (yearlings)

ROARING LION (USA) – grey 2015

Kitten's Joy (USA)	El Prado (IRE)	Sadler's Wells (USA)
		Lady Capulet (USA)
	Kitten's First (USA)	Lear Fan (USA)
		That's My Hon (USA)
Vionnet (USA)	Street Sense (USA)	Street Cry (IRE)
		Bedazzle (USA)
	Cambiocorsa (USA)	Avenue Of Flags (USA)
		Ultrafleet (USA)

TASLEET (GB)

Whitsbury Manor Stud stallion Showcasing (by Oasis Dream) has become one of the most sought-after sires in Britain following the emergence of a string of stakes and pattern winners from his first few crops, headed by dual Group 1 sprint star Quiet Reflection. His most recent batch of juveniles to race featured Group 1 Phoenix Stakes winner and Group 1 Dewhurst Stakes runner-up Advertise, and potential five-furlong star Soldier's Call. That colt took both the Group 2 Flying Childers Stakes and Listed Windsor Castle Stakes in England, won the Group 3 Prix d'Arenberg in France, and finished an honourable third to Mabs Cross and Gold Vibe in the Group 1 Prix de l'Abbaye de Longchamp in October, coming off worst in a three-way photo, but with Battaash – admittedly below his best – a half-length back in fourth.

His 32 stakes winners also include speedy juvenile Cappella Sansevero, a Compas Stallions horse standing at Bridge House Stud in Ireland and whose first yearlings made up to 140,000gns in 2018. He could do well as a freshman sire this year. Showcasing's second stallion son is also one of his most talented representatives, and Tasleet has joined the team at Nunnery Stud near Thetford in Norfolk, the base from where his famous great-grandsire Green Desert (by Danzig) founded a dynasty.

Tasleet's first blacktype success came in July of his juvenile year, he then chased home Shalaa in the Group 2 Richmond Stakes at Goodwood, won a valuable sales race, then lost out by a nose to Sanus Per Aquam in the Group 3 Sommerville Tattersall Stakes at Newmarket. He kicked off his three-year-old campaign in the Group 3 Greenham Stakes – which was run that year on the Polytrack at Chelmsford – and short-headed the subsequent Mehl-Mulhens-Rennen (German 2000 Guineas) scorer Knife Edge in that seven-furlong test. His only other outing that year was a disappointing unplaced finish behind Aclaim in the Group 2 Challenge Stakes in October, but he bounced back at four.

He was runner-up to Home Of The Brave in a seven-furlong listed contest on his return to action, then put up an excellent performance to trounce Magical Memory by two and a half lengths in the Group 2 Duke of York Stakes. This was his first run over six furlongs since that sales race at two, and it was the trip over which he ran every time for the rest of his career. The highlights were his neck second to The Tin Man in the Group 1 Diamond Jubilee Stakes at Royal Ascot, chasing home Harry Angel in the Group 1 32Red Sprint Cup on heavy ground at Haydock, taking the runners-up spot to Librisa Breeze in the Group 1 Qipco British Champions Sprint back at Ascot, and, at the age of five, finishing third to Merchant Navy in the Group 2 Weatherbys Ireland Greenlands Stakes at the Curragh.

Tasleet is the best of several winners out of Bird Key, an unraced Cadeaux Genereux (by Young Generation) half-sister to Group 2 Champagne Stakes winner and Group 1 July Cup third Etlaala (by Selkirk). Three of her other siblings were listed-placed, but the one that catches the eye is Anna Law (by Lawman). She showed little aptitude in a four-race career, but on his day, her son Battaash (by Dark Angel) is one of the most brilliant sprinters of the modern era.

His grandam Portelet (by Night Shift) won four times over the minimum trip, by an aggregate margin of 11 and a half lengths. Her dam Noirmant (by Dominion) was unraced, her half-sister Rozel (by Wolfhound) was runner-up in a listed sprint, and her grandam is the listed-placed dual winner Krakow (by Malinowski). That mare has appeared in the pedigree of many blacktype horses over the past three decades, and her roll of honour is headed by her son Braashee (by Sadler's Wells). He won the Group 1 Prix Royal-Oak, was third in the Group 1 Irish St Leger, and is a full-brother to multiple US Grade 3 scorer Adam Smith. Their half-sister Ghariba (by Final Straw) won the Group 3 Nell Gwyn Stakes and finished fourth in the Group 1 1000 Guineas at a time when that placing did count for blacktype, and is also notable for being the grandam of Group 3 winner and Group 1 Racing Post Trophy runner-up Fantastic View (by Distant View).

There are many more talented horses to be found if you go back another generation or two and examine their branches – including Group 1 scorers Bassenthwaite (by Habitat), Central Park (by In The Wings), Moon Ballad (by Singspiel), and Rebelline (by Robellino) – but those stars are so remote to Tasleet as to have no bearing on him or his potential. He looks sure to prove popular in his new role, seems likely to get his best winners in all age groups and to become a source of mostly sprinters and milers.

SUMMARY DETAILS

Standing: Nunnery Stud, Norfolk
Fee: £6,000
Career highlights: 5 wins inc Duke of York Clipper Logistics Stakes (Gr2), Betfred Greenham Stakes (Gr3), Compton Estates Rose Bowl Stakes (L), 2nd Diamond Jubilee Stakes (Gr1), Qipco British Champions Sprint Stakes (Gr1), 32Red Sprint Cup Stakes (Gr1), Qatar Richmond Stakes (Gr2), Somerville Tattersall Stakes (Gr3), Totepool EBF King Richard III Stakes (L), 3rd Weatherbys Ireland Greenlands Stakes (Gr2)
Other stallions by his sire include: Cappella Sansevero (2yo in 2019)

TASLEET (GB) – bay 2013

Showcasing (GB)	Oasis Dream (GB)	Green Desert (USA)
		Hope (IRE)
	Arabesque (GB)	Zafonic (USA)
		Prophecy (IRE)
Bird Key (GB)	Cadeaux Genereux	Young Generation
		Smarten Up
	Portelet (GB)	Night Shift (USA)
		Noirmant

UNFORTUNATELY (IRE)

Group 1-winning sprinter Society Rock (by Rock Of Gibraltar) was among the most popular new additions to the stallion ranks in 2014 and the Tally-Ho Stud-based horse sired 111 foals in his first crop. Sadly, he died in May of 2016. His first juveniles reached the track the following year, and the Karl Burke-trained Group 1 Prix Morny winner Unfortunately was the star among them.

That six-furlong feature was the colt's third win from six starts, it came a month after his half-length defeat of Frozen Angel in the Group 2 Prix Robert Papin over a half-furlong less at Maisons-Laffitte, and his three loses featured a head second in the Prix La Fleche over five at that same venue in June. The horse he beat at Deauville was his stablemate Havana Grey – previously a Group 3 scorer and subsequently also a winner at the highest level. The margin of victory was a length and a quarter, and the previously undefeated pattern-winning fillies Different League and Zonza were a short-head and short-neck back in third and fourth.

His only subsequent outing that year was in the Group 1 Middle Park Stakes in late September, but he disappointed and came home unplaced behind U S Navy Flag. His first four runs of 2018 were also a long way what he had shown in France, but he went out a winner – coincidentally on the anniversary of his Newmarket loss – when taking the Group 3 Renaissance Stakes over six furlongs at Naas. It was a much easier task than some of those he had faced during the season, but he got the job done and ended his track career on a high.

Unfortunately was bred by Tally-Ho Stud, he is a €24,000 graduate of the Tattersalls Ireland September Yearling Sale in Fairyhouse, and Timeform rated him 117 at two, which is a world away from what his dam achieved on the track. She was a plater who won two sellers – one of them at 40/1 – from 22 starts, earned a peak official handicap mark of 53 and finished her career with a well-beaten fourth over seven furlongs at Wolverhampton, off a mark of 43. Despite this limited talent,

Unfortunate (by Komaite) has done well as a broodmare and, in addition to her star son, she is the dam of the prolific fillies Red Roar (by Chineur; five wins), The City Kid (by Danetime; eight wins), and Look Busy (by Danetime). The last-named won a dozen times, including the Group 2 Temple Stakes, Group 3 Flying Five Stakes, and three listed contests, and her daughter Looks A Million (by Kyllachy) has been a stakes-placed winner over five furlongs.

Unfortunate is the only winner among seven foals out of Honour And Glory (by Hotfoot), and that unraced individual is out of Cheb's Honour (by Chebs Lad) who came up with six winners from 13 foals, one of whom was a talented sprinter. Singing Steven (by Balliol) won the Group 3 Cornwallis Stakes and Listed Harry Rosebery Challenge Trophy as a juvenile, went on to add the Group 3 King George Stakes over five furlongs at Goodwood, and sired winners from somewhat limited opportunities at stud.

Unfortunately, however, looks likely to be supported with large books because he is a juvenile Group 1 winner standing at one of the most famous studs in England. He seems likely to get sprinters and milers, and winners in all age groups. As for his late sire, Society Rock's offspring also include the pattern-placed sprint stakes winners Corinthia Knight and Shumookhi, Group 3 Jersey Stakes second Society Power, Group 3-placed juvenile Tangled, and high-class filly The Mackem Bullet. She lost out by a nose to Fairyland in the Group 2 Lowther Stakes and by a neck to that same rival in the Group 1 Cheveley Park Stakes last year.

SUMMARY DETAILS

Standing: Cheveley Park Stud, Newmarket
Fee: £7,500
Career highlights: 4 wins inc Darley Prix Morny (Gr1), Prix Robert Papin (Gr2), Renaissance Stakes (Gr3), 2nd Prix La Fleche (L)
Other stallions by his sire include: none

UNFORTUNATELY (IRE) – bay 2015

Society Rock (IRE)	Rock Of Gibraltar (IRE)	Danehill (USA)
		Offshore Boom
	High Society (IRE)	Key Of Luck (USA)
		Ela'a Gold (IRE)
Unfortunate (GB)	Komaite (USA)	Nureyev (USA)
		Brown Berry
	Honour And Glory (GB)	Hotfoot
		Cheb's Honour

WASHINGTON DC (IRE)

Washington DC represents the first crop of Zoffany (by Dansili), and he has joined the stallion ranks just as his sire's profile may be set to soar. That horse had an excellent year in 2018, seven of his stakes winners were two-year-olds, and they included Group 2 May Hill Stakes heroine Fleeting as well as Main Edition who won what turned out to be a strong edition of the Group 3 Albany Stakes at Royal Ascot. His earlier crops feature classic-placed Group 1 scorer Ventura Storm, triple Oaks-placed Architecture, three Group 1-placed Group 2 winners, and German Group 2 classic scorer Knife Edge, and the increased support that he attracted due to those results means that his more strongly bred offspring will start to appear on the track this year.

A late-April maiden winner at Tipperary on his second start at two, Washington DC was talented and durable in a career that spanned 32 races over four seasons, earning more than £500,000 in prize money. The Aidan O'Brien-trained bay was also widely travelled and often competed in Group 1 company, including in England, France, the United Arab Emirates, and in the USA. He was a stakes winner at two, three, and four years of age, Group 1-placed in both his first two seasons and his top effort at five was when chasing home Battaash in the Group 2 Temple Stakes at Haydock. He achieved his highest end-of-year Timeform rating as a three-year-old, and that mark of 121 equals that of his Group 1-winning sire.

The €340,000 he cost at the Goffs Orby Sale is a testament to his looks, and the presence of a classic sire in his family augurs well for his future.

Washington DC is the better of two winners out of the stakes-placed prolific sprinter How's She Cuttin' (by Shinko Forest), and he is inbred 4x4 to Danzig (by Northern Dancer). The mare is a half-sister to a listed-placed horse, but more notable is that her siblings include Manuka Magic (by Key Of Luck), the dam of Group 3 Firth of Clyde Stakes winner and

Group 1 Cheveley Park Stakes third Aspen Darlin (by Indian Haven). Her third dam is the classic-placed Cheveley Park Stakes winner Magic Flute (by Tudor Melody), and although that five-time scorer was the dam of two listed winners, it is the record of her daughter La Papagena (by Habitat) that catches the eye.

Her daughters include the stakes winners and blacktype producers La Persiana (by Daylami) and Papabile (by Chief's Crown), her descendants feature dual Australian filly champion English (by Encosta De Lago), but her star son is Grand Lodge (by Chief's Crown), and like Washington DC, he represents the Danzig sire line. He was Europe's champion two-year-old of 1993 following his victory in the Group 1 Dewhurst Stakes, and he was again one of the top horses at three. He won the Group 1 St James's Palace Stakes, was runner-up in the Group 1 2000 Guineas and Group 1 Dubai Champion Stakes at Newmarket, and took third in both the Group 1 Sussex Stakes at Goodwood and Group 1 Irish Champion Stakes at Leopardstown. Timeform rated him 125.

Grand Lodge was a Coolmore shuttle stallion who sired 63 stakes winners, a dozen of whom won at least once at the highest level. He was only 12 when he died, and the most brilliant of his offspring was H.H. the Aga Khan's homebred Sinndar, the John Oxx-trained, Timeform 134-rated champion who beat Sakhee in the Derby, stormed home by nine lengths in the Irish Derby, ran away with the Group 2 Prix Niel, and then beat Egyptband, Volvoreta and Montjeu in the Group 1 Prix de l'Arc de Triomphe. Sinndar went on to become a classic sire, and he died last year at the age of 21.

Washington DC had the mixture of precocity and speed that many love, and also the durability that too many lack, plus he is a Danehill-line horse from the family of a leading international sire. All of this makes him a promising prospect who should get his best winners in all age groups, mostly sprinters, but some of whom may stay a mile.

SUMMARY DETAILS

Standing: Bearstone Stud, Shropshire

Fee: £6,000

Career highlights: 6 wins inc At The Races Phoenix Sprint Stakes (Gr3), Woodlands Stakes (L), Coolmore Stud Power Committed Stakes (L), Paddy Power Patton Stakes (L), Windsor Castle Stakes (L), 2nd Qatar Prix de l'Abbaye de Longchamp (Gr1), Keeneland Phoenix Stakes (Gr1), Derrinstown Stud Flying Five Stakes (Gr2), Qatar King George Stakes (Gr2), Armstrong Aggregates Temple Stakes (Gr2), Bar One Racing Lacken Stakes (Gr3), Longholes Palace House Stakes (Gr3), Cold Move EBF Marble Hill Stakes (L), 3rd Commonwealth Cup (Gr1), Woodlands Stakes (L)

Other stallions by his sire include: none

WASHINGTON DC (IRE) – bay 2013

Zoffany (IRE)	Dansili (GB)	Danehill (USA)
		Hasili (IRE)
	Tyranny (GB)	Machiavellian (USA)
		Dust Dancer (GB)
How's She Cuttin' (IRE)	Shinko Forest (IRE)	Green Desert (USA)
		Park Express
	Magic Annemarie (IRE)	Dancing Dissident (USA)
		Magic Garter

ZOUSTAR (AUS)

Zoustar is new to stud in Europe in 2019, and he will be listed as a freshman sire here in 2022, but unlike his cohorts he is already an established Australian stallion whose first crop, born in the latter half of 2015, has thus far yielded six stakes winners, headed by Group 1-winning sprinter Sunlight and the Group 1-placed Group 2 scorers Lean Mean Machine and Zouzain. His second crop, currently juveniles 'down under', features Group 3 winner Sun City. This is a highly promising start to his career, and while every other stallion covering their first European book in 2019 is currently an unknown quantity, there is a different question to be asked with this horse. It is not a matter of whether or not he has the potential to sire top horses – he has already done that – but, instead, will he click with the European mares?

There have been quite a few Australian stallions who failed to replicate their local success here, just as there have been some notable northern hemisphere sires who fared poorly during their shuttle seasons. However, there have also been success stories such as Choisir, Exceed And Excel, and Fastnet Rock, and hopefully Zoustar can become another.

He is one of six Group 1 winners among the 24 stakes winners by Northern Meteor, a Group 1-winning sprinter who died at the age of seven. That much-lamented horse was a grandson of Sadler's Wells's full-brother Fairy King, but although his 14 top-level winners among 73 blacktype scorers featured European classic winners such as Oath (Derby) and Turtle Island (Irish 2000 Guineas), Fairy King's sons were generally poor as stallions. The notable exception was Encosta De Lago who was an outstanding sire in Australia, getting 26 Group 1 stars among an overall total of 115 stakes winners, and it is he who gave us Northern Meteor.

Zoustar is the best of three winners out of one-time scorer Zouzou (by Redoute's Choice), and it catches the eye that the mare moved to Ireland a few years ago. She has a three-year-old filly named At Last, she had colts in 2017 and 2018, and all three are by prolific champion sire Galileo (by Sadler's Wells). At Last is trained by Aidan O'Brien, she was unplaced in a one-mile Cork maiden in August on what was her only start at two, and she holds an entry in the Group 1 Darley Irish Oaks. With Zoustar being a sprinter who was Group 1-placed over a mile, and his best early runners showing speed, one wonders if perhaps his Galileo-sired siblings may be mile-to-10-furlong horses rather than ones who will be effective over farther.

Meteor Mist (by Star Shower), his grandam, was also a capable sprinter-miler, and although she did not earn any blacktype, she won 12 times on the track and produced four winners from five foals at stud, one of them being multiple blacktype-placed seven-time scorer Crestfallen (by Rivotious). That filly went on to produce several successful offspring, she has a stakes-placed daughter by leading sire I Am Invincible (by Invincible Spirit), and she is the grandam of Group 2-placed stakes winner Testashadow (by Testa Rossa), an eight-time scorer at seven and eight furlongs. Crestfallen's winning half-sister Forever Midnight (by Snippets) has also done her part for the family as she is the dam of the Group 2-winning sprinter Dusty Star (by General Nediym).

There are some speedy blacktype-placed sprinters under a branch of the third generation of the pedigree, and third dam Sunbuster (by Blockbuster) – who won over four and a half furlongs – is a half-sister to the dam of Group 3 scorer Diamond Benny (by Hit It Benny), but there is nothing that hints at why Zoustar has done so well as a stallion. He is not the first by his sire to stand here. The well-related Group 1 star Shooting To Win served a single season at Kildangan Stud, but covered just 35 mares, got 24 foals, and is a freshman sire in 2019. In Australia, however, that horse has a large first juvenile crop, and from a handful of runners at the time of writing, he is off the mark with his first winner, a filly.

Being a proven Group 1 sire, Zoustar looks sure to attract plenty of support in his first European season. Hopefully, he will prove just as successful here as he is in the southern hemisphere. He has Fairy King, Fappiano (by Mr Prospector) and Danehill (by Danzig) in the third generation of his chart –

which should boost his prospects of being compatible with our bloodlines – yet his pedigree offers something a bit different, and we need that too.

SUMMARY DETAILS

Standing: Tweenhills Farm & Stud, Gloucestershire
Fee: £25,000
Career highlights: 6 wins inc Golden Rose Stakes (Gr1), VRC Coolmore Stud Stakes (Gr1), Roman Consul Stakes (Gr2), BRC Sires' Produce Stakes (Gr2), 2nd BRC JJ Atkins Stakes (Gr1)
Other stallions by his sire include: Eurozone (L), Fighting Sun (L), Deep Field (winners), Shooting To Win (winners; 2yo in 2019)

ZOUSTAR (AUS) – bay 2010

Northern Meteor (AUS)	Encosta De Lago (AUS)	Fairy King (USA)
		Shoal Creek (AUS)
	Explosive (USA)	Fappiano (USA)
		Scuff (USA)
Zouzou (AUS)	Redoute's Choice (AUS)	Danehill (USA)
		Shantha's Choice (AUS)
	Meteor Mist (AUS)	Star Shower (AUS)
		Sunbuster (AUS)

FRANCE

CHANDUCOQ (FR)

He only won once, and he picked up some blacktype when third in a listed juvenile hurdle, but Chanducoq is a horse who could become well-known a few years from now. He is a new National Hunt stallion for 2019 and one with the potential to do well in that role.

The first thing that stands out in his pedigree is that he is a son of the much lamented Voix Du Nord and out of a mare who represents a Nikos - Cadoudal cross. Those are strong National Hunt lines. His sire died aged 12, but the Group 1-winning son of the top-class Lomond (by Northern Dancer) horse Valanour left behind an array of notable jumpers, a roll of honour that includes Vroum Vroum Mag, Taquin De Seuil, Vibrato Valtat, Defi Du Seuil, Vaniteux, Vieux Morvan, Bachasson, Val De Ferbet, and rising star Kemboy who was such an impressive winner of the Grade 1 Savills Chase over three miles at Leopardstown in late December.

Voix Du Nord's talented representatives also include triple Grade 3-winning hurdler Caesar's Palace, and that gelding is Chanducoq's older full-brother. Their half-brother Cesare Di Roma (by No Risk At All) was listed-placed over hurdles last year, but their siblings also include Cokoriko (by Robin Des Champs), a blacktype-winning hurdler who stands at Haras de Cercy and is one of the most popular young stallions in France. Those in his first crop have just turned four, yet they already include the Grade 2-winning chaser Polirico and listed hurdles scorer Flying Startandco, as well as the Grade 3-placed Etoile Du Ficheaux. His fee has trebled in 2019, to €6,000.

Chanducoq's winning dam Cardounika is out three-time scorer Cardoudalle, a mare who has had six winners from nine runners. It is, however, two of her non-winners who deserve mention and that is because they have become broodmares of note. Cardamine (by Garde Royale), who was unplaced, is the dam of Corscia (by Nickname) – a dual Grade 3 heroine over hurdles and also over fences – and of listed hurdle winner Calotin (by Martaline). Cana (by Robin Des Champs), on the other hand, is the dam of Benie Des Dieux (by Great Pretender). She was a Grade 3-placed hurdler when trained in France but is unbeaten in five starts since joining the Willie Mullins stable in Ireland. She won by 30 lengths first time out over fences, added listed chase success at Carlisle and Naas, then switched to the smaller obstacles at the 2018 Cheltenham Festival and won the Grade 1 OLBG Mares' Hurdle over two and a half miles. Then she added the Grade 1 Irish Stallion Farms EBF Annie Power Mares Champion Hurdle over the same trip at the Punchestown Festival a month and a half later.

Chanducoq's third dam, Easy Horse (by Carmarthen), is a winning full-sister to the talented hurdlers Dazzling Horse and Funny Horse and a half-sister to the smart chaser Sweet Virginia (by Tapioca), which highlights how this is a family long associated with National Hunt success. He looks sure to prove popular in his new role, especially if his half-brother's run of success continues, and it would be no surprise to see him become a National Hunt sire of note in the coming years.

SUMMARY DETAILS
Standing: Haras de la Barbottière
Fee: €1,400
Career highlights: 1 win inc 3rd Prix Andre Massena Grande Course de Haies des 4 Ans (NH-L)
Other stallions by his sire include: Robin Du Nord (3yo in 2019)

CHANDUCOQ (FR) – bay 2013

Voix Du Nord (FR)	Valanour (IRE)	Lomond (USA)
		Vearia
	Dame Edith (FR)	Top Ville
		Girl Of France
Cardounika (FR)	Nikos	Nonoalco (USA)
		No No Nanette (FR)
	Cardoudalle (FR)	Cadoudal (FR)
		Easy Horse (FR)

CHEMICAL CHARGE (IRE)

Sea The Stars (by Cape Cross) wasted no time in establishing himself as one of the most important sires in Europe, and as you would expect, there is a growing number of his sons going to stud. These include the former Ger Lyons and Ralph Beckett-trained Chemical Charge, a pattern-winning middle-distance horse who earned a Timeform rating of 120. He was effective on turf and on Polytrack, his Group 3 win came over 12 furlongs on the latter, and in addition to his many pieces of blacktype, it is worth noting that he finished a two-and-three-quarter-length fourth to Highland Reel in the Group 1 Longines Hong Kong Vase at Sha Tin.

He won both his starts as a juvenile, he is a full-brother to a multiple winner, and he comes from one of the most famous stallion-producing families of recent decades. His stakes-placed dam, Jakonda (by Kingmambo), won over 10 and a half furlongs, she is a half-sister to two blacktype-placed multiple scorers, and she is out of Mystery Trip (by Belong To Me), an unraced daughter of Weekend Surprise (by Secretariat). That Grade 1-placed dual Grade 3 winner is the dam of classic star and leading sire Summer Squall (by Storm Bird), multiple Group/Grade 1 sire Honor Grades (by Danzig), and US Horse of the Year and dynasty-making stallion A.P. Indy (by Seattle Slew), who is still fine fettle, in retirement from active service, at his long-time home Lane's End Farm in Kentucky, now aged 30.

Weekend Surprise is also the dam of the stakes-winning pair Eavesdropper (by Kingmambo) and Welcome Surprise (by Seeking The Gold), and the many blacktype scorers who descend from her include Court Vision (by Gulch). His five Grade 1 wins featured the Breeders' Cup Mile, and he has sired stakes winners and a juvenile champion in Canada. The mare was herself a half-sister to Group 1 winner Wolfhound (by Nureyev; sire of Group 1 winner Bright Sky), to blacktype scorer and sire Foxhound (by Danzig; sire of Group 1 scorer Mount Abu), to Deerhound (by Danzig; sire of Grade 1 winner Countess Diana), to Spectacular Spy (by Spectacular Bid; sire of Australian Group 1 scorer Quick Flick), and to Al Mufti (by Roberto), a champion sire in South Africa.

This means that the fourth dam of Chemical Charge is Lassie Dear (by Buckpasser). A winner of five of her 26 starts, including a Grade 3 contest, she was out of Grade 1 Ashland Stakes heroine Gay Missile (by Sir Gaylord). This made her a half-sister to Group 1 Grand Prix de Saint-Cloud winner and leading French sire Gay Mecene (by Vaguely Noble), and also to Gallanta (by Nureyev), the Group 1-placed, stakes-winning dam of Gay Gallanta (by Woodman) and Sportsworld (by Alleged). The former is the Group 1 winning dam of Gordon Lord Byron's sire Byron (by Green Desert), while the latter was a leading sire in South Africa.

All of the above would be more than enough to illustrate the genetic legacy that Chemical Charge represents, but as they say in the commercials – there's more. Lassie Dear's daughters also included Charming Lassie (by Seattle Slew) and stakes-placed Lassie's Lady (by Alydar). The former is the dam of Group 3 Coventry Stakes winner and Group 1 Sussex Stakes runner-up Statue Of Liberty (by Storm Cat; sire of three-time Australian Group 1 scorer Hay List) and of the champion and prolific US Grade 1 star Lemon Drop Kid (by Kingmambo), a leading sire in North America. Lassie's Lady, on the other hand, had a couple of stakes-winning sons of her own, but it is two of her grandsons who stand out: multiple Group 1 ace Duke Of Marmalade (by Danehill) and his Derby-winning half-brother Ruler Of The World (by Galileo).

Duke Of Marmalade did not make as quick a start to his stallion career as would have been hoped, and he was exported to South Africa, but Europe's loss is that country's gain as the now Drakenstein Stud resident left behind Big Orange, Nutan, Simple Verse, Sound Of Freedom, and Star Of Seville – all Group 1 winners. Ruler Of The World's first crop was neither as big nor as popular as might have been expected, but they include Group 1 Fillies' Mile heroine and leading Oaks candidate Iridessa. The young Coolmore stallion's best results are likely to be seen when his offspring try middle-distances.

If it were just a matter of pedigree – and it's not, of course – then Chemical Charge would odds-on to do well in his new career, mostly with middle-distance horses and stayers. Much will depend on the level of the support that he receives, and on the physical qualities that he passes on, and it seems likely that he will attract the attention of both flat and National Hunt breeders.

SUMMARY DETAILS

Standing: Haras de Grandcamp
Fee: €4,000
Career highlights: 5 wins inc toteplacepot September Stakes (Gr3), 2nd Finlay Volvo International Stakes (Gr3), Prix Max Sicard (L), 32Red Wild Flower Stakes (L), Lenebane Stakes (L), TRI Equestrian Silver Stakes (L), 3rd Hardwicke Stakes (Gr2),
Other stallions by his sire include: Sea The Moon (Gr3), Affinisea (yearlings in 2019), Harzand (yearlings), Storm The Stars (foals), Zelzal (foals)

CHEMICAL CHARGE (IRE) – chestnut 2012

Sea The Stars (IRE)	Cape Cross (IRE)	Green Desert (USA)
		Park Appeal
	Urban Sea (USA)	Miswaki (USA)
		Allegretta
Jakonda (USA)	Kingmambo (USA)	Mr Prospector (USA)
		Miesque (USA)
	Mystery Trip (USA)	Belong To Me (USA)
		Weekend Surprise (USA)

CLOTH OF STARS (IRE)

Having achieved the rarely seen Timeform rating of 140, it is unlikely that even a sire of the calibre of Sea The Stars (by Cape Cross) will get a son as good as he was, although it is possible, of course. Cloth Of Stars made it to a mark of 132 following a four-year-old campaign that saw him win the Group 1 Prix Ganay, Group 2 Prix d'Harcourt, and Group 3 Prix Exbury, and chase home Enable in the Group 1 Qatar Prix de l'Arc de Triomphe. He was still top-class at five, albeit dropping to 128, and it was something of a surprise that he failed to win in 2018, notching up a string of placed efforts instead, including a third-place finish to Enable and Sea Of Class in another Arc.

He was a Group 1-placed pattern winner over a mile as a juvenile, he won both the Group 2 Prix Greffulhe and Group 3 Prix La Force at three, and another highlight of that season was his third-place finish in the Group 1 Juddmonte Grand Prix de Paris at Saint-Cloud. Now this earner of over £2.5 million in prize money is embarking on a new career as a Darley sire at Haras du Logis. The first stallion son of Sea The Stars is the runaway Group 1 Deutsches Derby hero Sea The Moon, and that Lanwades Stud resident made an eye-catching start as a freshman sire in 2018 with a double-digit tally of winners, two of whom were Group 3 scorers and another two placed in blacktype company.

Cloth Of Stars is one of three sons of Sea The Stars who have joined the stallion ranks in France in 2019 – Chemical Charge and Mekhtaal are the other two. His dam did not win, she is the Kingmambo (by Mr Prospector) mare Strawberry Fledge, and she is a full-sister to Group 1 Oaks heroine Light Shift. That star also has a son at stud as her King George and Arc-placed dual 10-furlong Group 1 star Ulysses (by Galileo) is part of the team at Cheveley Park Stud in Newmarket, with his first foals arriving this year.

Light Shift's half-sister Shiva (by Hector Protector) won the Group 1 Tattersalls Gold Cup and produced the Group 2-

placed French listed scorer That Which Is Not (by Elusive Quality). She is also a half-sister to Burning Sunset (by Caerleon), who is the Group 2-placed, stakes-winning dam of Group 1-placed, Group 2 Prix d'Harcourt winner Smoking Sun (by Smart Strike), and that mare is also notable as being the grandam of US champion and multiple Grade 1 star Main Sequence (by Aldebaran) who chased home Camelot in the Group 1 Derby at Epsom in 2012.

Light Shift's siblings also include the talented middle-distance horse Limnos (by Hector Protector), who won the Group 2 Prix Foy and Group 2 Prix Jean de Chaudennay, and Molasses (by Machiavellian), a non-winner who became the dam of Group 3 Prix d'Hedouville winner and Group 1 Grand Prix de Paris third Magadan (by High Chaparral). Her dam did not win either – Lingerie (by Shirley Heights) was placed – but her grandam is 1984's European champion three-year-old filly Northern Trick (by Northern Dancer), winner of the Group 3 Prix de la Nonette, Group 1 Prix de Diane (French Oaks), and Group 1 Prix Vermeille before chasing home Sagace in the Arc. She finished that year on a Timeform rating of 131, and her descendants also include a pair of Grade 1-winning half-brothers in Brazil: Jeune-Turc (by Know Heights; sire of a Grade 1 winner) and Nonno Luigi (by Dubai Dust).

With a family of this strength and depth behind him, it is no surprise that Cloth Of Stars became a top-class racehorse. He was a pattern winner at two, three, and four years of age, Group 1-placed in all four of his seasons on the track, twice placed in the Arc, and a winner once at the highest level. He looks sure to prove popular in his new role, and he has the potential to become a notable sire of milers, middle-distance horses and stayers in the years to come.

SUMMARY DETAILS

Standing: Haras du Logis
Fee: €7,500
Career highlights: 7 wins inc Prix Ganay (Gr1), Prix d'Harcourt (Gr2), Prix Greffulhe (Gr2), Prix Exbury (Gr3), Prix La Force (Gr3), Prix des Chenes (Gr3), 2nd Qatar Prix de

l'Arc de Triomphe (Gr1), Criterium de Saint-Cloud (Gr1), Qatar Prix Foy (Gr2), 3rd Qatar Prix de l'Arc de Triomphe (Gr1), Longines Dubai Sheema Classic (Gr1), Prix Ganay l'Inauguration de ParisLongchamp (Gr1), Juddmonte Grand Prix de Paris (Gr1), Qatar Prix Foy (Gr2), Prix de Conde (Gr3) **Other stallions by his sire include:** Sea The Moon (Gr3), Affinisea (yearlings in 2019), Harzand (yearlings), Storm The Stars (foals), Zelzal (foals)

CLOTH OF STARS (IRE) – bay 2013

Sea The Stars (IRE)	Cape Cross (IRE)	Green Desert (USA)
		Park Appeal
	Urban Sea (USA)	Miswaki (USA)
		Allegretta
Strawberry Fledge (USA)	Kingmambo (USA)	Mr Prospector (USA)
		Miesque (USA)
	Lingerie (GB)	Shirley Heights
		Northern Trick (USA)

DOHA DREAM (FR)

Doha Dream was a short-head winner of the Group 2 Qatar Prix Chaudennay over 15 furlongs at Chantilly in October 2016, and from the moment the result of that photo finish was called, it was probably a shade of odds-on that he would eventually find a place at stud. Previously a Group 2-placed dual stakes winner, and subsequently narrowly beaten in a Group 2 and pair of Group 3s, the son of Shamardal (by Giant's Causeway) comes from a famous stallion-producing family. His appeal is likely to lie mainly within the National Hunt sector, and it is to there that his paternal half-brother Casamento has moved following a promising start with his first bumper runners and hurdlers. That horse is now at Sunnyhill Stud in Ireland.

Shamardal's son Captain Sonador died young but has had a top-level winner in Hong Kong. Nunnery Stud resident Mukhadram got a stakes winner in his first crop of two-year-olds in 2018, and several others have got winners, but most of the sons of the Kildangan Stud standout are in early stages of their stallion careers, with several due to be represented by their first juveniles in the coming months. The eldest and most notable of them, however, is well-established as a leading international sire.

Dual classic star Lope De Vega heads the roster at Ballylinch Stud in Ireland, and his 52 stakes winners feature seven who have won at least once at the highest level. Those Group/Grade 1 wins have come in Australia, Canada, England, France, the United Arab Emirates, and the USA, his classic horses include two who have made the frame in the Irish 2000 Guineas, and his champion son Belardo will have yearlings on offer this summer and autumn. Indeed, Lope De Vega's profile looks set to rise even higher as an increasing fee and increasing support led to an outstanding 2018 for him, especially with his two-year-olds. Seven of those won listed or pattern events, headed by unbeaten Newspaperofrecord's impressive Grade 1 Breeders' Cup Juvenile Fillies Turf success.

131

Doha Dream is out of Crystal Reef (by King's Best), a non-winning half-sister to three horses of note. Reefscape (by Linamix) won the Group 1 Prix du Cadran, proved to be almost sterile and was gelded, but the handful of foals he sired included the Grade 1-winning mare L'Unique. Haras de Cercy stallion Coastal Path (by Halling) was also a talented stayer, and the Group 2 scorer's early offspring include the high-class Bacardys. The third one is Group 2 Prix Maurice de Nieuil winner and leading National Hunt sire Martaline (by Linamix). The Haras de Montaigu resident is responsible for Dynaste, Ucello Conti, Agrapart, Edward D'Argent, Kotkikova, Disko, and many others of note.

Coraline (by Sadler's Wells), the winning grandam of Doha Dream, is a half-sister to Group 1 Irish Oaks star Wemyss Bight (by Dancing Brave) and so can be described as being a three-parts sister to multiple Group/Grade 1 scorer and good dual-purpose sire Beat Hollow (by Sadler's Wells). Her siblings also include the dams of high-class stayer Bellamy Cay (by Kris), sprint champion and outstanding flat sire Oasis Dream (by Green Desert), and Zenda (by Zamindar), the classic-winning dam of brilliant miler Kingman (by Invincible Spirit). He made an excellent start to his stallion career in 2018 with a string of stakes winners among a double-digit tally of first-crop juvenile winners.

Coraline's full-sister to Trellis Bay, who is the dam of Bellamy Cay, is also notable as being the grandam of Arc-placed Group 1 Prix du Jockey Club (French Derby) star New Bay (by Dubawi), the young Ballylinch Stud stallion whose first foals were well received in the auction ring last year.

All of this makes Doha Dream an interesting new addition to the stallion ranks, and he has the potential to make a name for himself as a National Hunt sire.

SUMMARY DETAILS

Standing: Haras du Hoguenet
Fee: €2,500
Career highlights: 5 wins inc Qatar Prix Chaudenay (Gr2), Prix Frederic de Lagrange (L), Derby de l'Ouest-Haras du Saz

(L), 2nd Luciene Barriere Grand Prix de Deauville (Gr2),
Haras de la Pomme Prix de Reux (Gr3), Prix de Barbeville
(Gr3), Coupe des Trois Ans (L), 3rd Qatar Prix Niel (Gr2)
Other stallions by his sire include: Captain Sonador (Gr1),
Lope De Vega (Gr1), Casamento (Gr2), Mukhadram (L),
Shamoline Warrior (L), Ghibellines (winners), Gingerbread
Man (winners), Shakespearean (winners), Sommerabend
(winners), Amaron (2yo in 2019), Crackerjack King (2yo),
French Navy (2yo), Zazou (2yo), Bow Creek (yearlings),
Dariyan (yearlings), Lightning Moon (yearlings), Balios (foals)

DOHA DREAM (FR) – bay 2013

Shamardal (USA)	Giant's Causeway (USA)	Storm Cat (USA)
		Mariah's Storm (USA)
	Helsinki (GB)	Machiavellian (USA)
		Helen Street
Crystal Reef (GB)	King's Best (USA)	Kingmambo (USA)
		Allegretta
	Coraline (GB)	Sadler's Wells (USA)
		Bahamian

DSCHINGIS SECRET (GER)

Prolific pattern winner Soldier Hollow (by In The Wings) won four Group 1s over 10 furlongs, the last of them a three-length score in the Grosser Dallmayr-Preis Bayerisches Zuchtrennen at Munich as a seven-year-old, and he has gone on to become one of the leading sires in Germany. He stands at Gestut Auenquelle, his fee for this year was €30,000, and his stakes winners include the classic stars Pastorius, Serienholde, and Weltstar, as well as additional Group 1 winners Ivanhowe (ran in Australia as Our Ivanhowe) and Dschingis Secret.

The latter achieved that feat, and he beat Hawkbill by a length in the Group 1 Longines Grosser Preis von Berlin over 12 furlongs at Hoppegarten in the summer of 2017. This came after a three-and-three-quarter-length defeat of Iquitos in the Group 2 Hansa Preis over the same trip at Hamburg. Earlier that season, he beat Sirius by six lengths in the Group 2 Gerling-Preis over a mile and a half at Cologne and at three he was a half-length third to Isfahan in the Group 1 Deutsches Derby and an eased-down seven-length winner of the Group 3 St Leger Italiano over 14 furlongs at San Siro.

A month after his top-level victory, he confirmed his status as a serious contender for the Group 1 Qatar Prix de l'Arc de Triomphe by beating Cloth Of Stars and Talismanic by a length and a half and a neck in the Group 2 Qatar Prix Foy over the 12 furlongs at Chantilly, with Satono Diamond fourth and Silverwave fifth. He ran well in the main event, coming home a seven-length sixth to Enable, and then had to settle for third in the Group 1 Grosser Preis von Bayern at Munich, beaten a neck and a neck by Guignol and Iquitos, with Waldgeist fourth. Timeform rated him 125.

He was not quite as good in 2018, but he chased home Waldgeist in the Group 2 Grand Prix de Chantilly in May, picked up a second edition of the Group 2 Grosser Hansa-Preis at Hamburg in early July, and then finished fourth to Best Solution in the Group 1 Grosser Preis von Berlin, beaten a total of one and three-quarter lengths. He was unplaced behind that same rival on his final start.

Dschingis Secret, a €200,000 graduate of the BBAG September Yearling Sale, is a full-brother to 2018's 12-furlong pattern scorer and narrow Group 1 Deutsches Derby runner-up Destino, to the dual pattern-placed filly Diana Storm, and to Dschingis First, a Markus Klug-trained colt who was Group 3-placed over eight and a half furlongs at Krefeld in early November. That three-year-old, who made €500,000 in Baden-Baden as a yearling, could be another classic contender for the family in 2019.

His dam, Divya (by Platini), won three times at four and five years of age and she is a full-sister to Deva, the dual 10-furlong Group 3-winning dam of Devastar (by Areion), who won the 10-furlong Group 3 Preis der Deutschen Einheit last year. Deva is also the grandam of 2015 Group 3 Preis der Winterkonigin heroine and German juvenile filly champion Dhaba (by Areion), she is a half-sister to a couple of stakes winners, and out of Diana's Quest (by Rainbow Quest), a winning daughter of the Canadian-born Diana Dance (by Northern Dancer). That Windfields Farm-bred mare also raced in Germany, where she was a Group 3 scorer over 10 and a half furlongs, runner-up in the Group 2 ARAG-Preis (German 1000 Guineas) and third in the Group 2 Preis der Diana (German Oaks).

A half-sister to Canadian juvenile filly champion Deceit Dancer (by Vice Regent) and to Grade 2 scorer and Japanese stallion Nagurski (by Nijinsky) – the sire of ill-fated champion Hokuto Vega – Diana Dance died young but was responsible for the prolific gelding Dorlando (by Kris) whose double-digit tally of wins was backed up by several blacktype placings in sprints. Deceit (by Prince John), the fourth dam of Dschingis Secret, was a prolific stakes winner from five and a half to nine and a half furlongs, with a tally that featured the Acorn Stakes, Mother Goose Stakes, and Matchmaker Stakes. Others of note in the family include the Grade 1 La Brea Stakes heroine Magical Allure (by General Meeting), who was out of a half-sister to Deceit.

Dschingis Secret is among the best German horses of recent years, and this Group 1-winning great-grandson of Sadler's Wells (by Northern Dancer) is likely to prove popular in his new role, both as a potential sire of middle-distance horses and stayers on the flat and within the of National Hunt sector.

SUMMARY DETAILS

Standing: Haras de Saint Arnoult
Fee: €4,000
Career highlights: 7 wins inc 127th Longines Grosser Preis von Berlin (Gr1), pferdewetten.de - Grosser Hansa-Preis (Gr2-twice), Qatar Prix Foy (Gr2), Gerling Preis (Gr2), St Leger Italiano (Gr3), 2nd Grand Prix de Chantilly (Gr2), 3rd Pastorius - Grosser Preis von Bayern (Gr1), Idee 147th Deutsches Derby (Gr1), Oppenheim-Union-Rennen (Gr2), Grosser Preis der Hannoverschen Volksbank - Derby Trial (L)
Other stallions by his sire include: Pastorius (winners), Ivanhowe (foals)

DSCHINGIS SECRET (GER) – bay 2013

Soldier Hollow (GB)	In The Wings	Sadler's Wells (USA)
		High Hawk
	Island Race (GB)	Common Grounds
		Lake Isle (IRE)
Divya (GER)	Platini (GER)	Surumu (GER)
		Prairie Darling
	Diana's Quest (IRE)	Rainbow Quest (USA)
		Diana Dance (CAN)

GUIGNOL (GER)

A triple middle-distance Group 1 winner who achieved a rating of 124 from Timeform as a five-year-old, Guignol is by the sire of Sea The Stars and out of a classic-winning full-sister to a rising star in the National Hunt stallion ranks. He looks likely to prove popular in his new role and to become a sire of talented middle-distance horses, stayers, and National Hunt winners.

He did not race at two, the horse he beat by a neck in an 11-furlong maiden on his debut at three was subsequent Group 1 Deutsches Derby scorer Nutan, and he picked up his first top-level placings the following year, taking third to Protectionist in the Grosser Preis von Berlin a month and a half before beating Racing History, Hawkbill, and Iquitos in the Grosser Preis von Bayern at Munich, both over 12 furlongs. He made all in that last contest and won by one and three-quarter lengths. He was unplaced behind Cloth Of Stars in the Group 1 Prix Ganay over 10 and a half furlongs at Saint-Cloud on his seasonal reappearance at five but bounced back to beat Iquitos in a Group 2 over a half-furlong farther at Baden-Baden. That Group 1 star was also his immediate victim in both the top-level races he won later that autumn.

First, he landed the Grosser Preis von Baden by two and a half lengths on good ground in early September, with that year's Group 1 Deutsches Derby winner Windstoss another length away in fourth. Then he added a repeat success in the Group 1 Grosser Preis von Bayern, this time winning by a neck, with Dschingis Secret the same margin back in third and a gap of one and a half lengths to fourth-placed French raider Waldgeist. He made the running in both. An ambitious tilt at the Group 1 Japan Cup, in which he faced firm ground for the only time in his career, did not pay off and he finished ninth to Cheval Grand.

Guignol returned to training in 2018 but ran just once, finishing third to Iquitos and Walsingham in the Group 2 Grosser Preis der Badenischen Wirtschaft over 11 furlongs on good ground at Baden-Baden in early June. Unlike so many of his previous starts, he was not able to get to the front until two out, a lead that he only held for around a furlong.

The son of late Group 1-winning miler and leading classic sire Cape Cross (by Green Desert) is out of the high-class middle-distance performer Guadalupe (by Monsun), and that makes him a half-brother to Guiliani (by Tertullian), a 10-furlong Group 1 scorer who was also talented at a mile. That horse began his stallion career at Gestut Schlenderhan, those in his first crop are yearlings, and he is at Gestut Erftmuhle in 2019. Their dam won the Group 1 Oaks d'Italia, was runner-up in the Group 1 Yorkshire Oaks and Group 1 Gran Premio del Jockey Club, third in the Group 1 Preis der Diana (German Oaks), and fourth in the Group 1 Prix Vermeille, and she was joint-champion three-year-old filly in Germany in 2002. She was also responsible for Guantana (by Dynaformer), who is the pattern-placed, stakes-winning dam of Group 2 Gerling Preis scorer Guardini (by Dalakhani), and she was crowned Broodmare of the Year in Germany in 2016.

Guadalupe's success at stud is no surprise, because in addition to being a classic-winning daughter of the outstanding German stallion Monsun (by Konigsstuhl), she is out of Guernica (by Unfuwain). That half-sister to Group 1 Gold Cup scorer Royal Rebel (by Robellino) is the dam of the dual Group 2-placed, blacktype-winning stayer Guadalajara (by Acatenango) and, more notable, French and dual German champion Getaway. He is a full-brother to Guadalupe, he won the Group 1 Deutschland Preis, Group 1 Grosser Preis von Baden, Group 2 Prix Kergorlay, Group 2 Jockey Club Stakes, and Group 2 Grand Prix de Deauville, and he is one of the most sought-after National Hunt stallions in Ireland. He stands at Coolmore's Grange Stud, and his first crop daughter Verdana Blue gave him an initial Grade 1 winner in late December when pipping dual Champion Hurdle hero Buveur d'Air in the Christmas Hurdle at Kempton. His first crop son Getabird, who easily won a pair of Grade 2 contests as a novice hurdler, was a half-length runner-up in a Grade 1 novice chase at Leopardstown that same day. The stallion's second crop includes the lightly raced Getaway Katie Mai who won the Grade 2 mares' bumper at Aintree last April and her maiden hurdle at Tramore in December.

Given his combination of pedigree and race record, Guignol's stallion potential is clear. It will be interesting to see what sort of support he attracts in the early years, and it would be no surprise to see him come up with blacktype winners under both codes.

SUMMARY DETAILS

Standing: Haras d'Annebault
Fee: €4,500
Career highlights: 6 wins inc Pastorius - Grosser Preis von Bayern (Gr1-twice), 145th Longines Grosser Preis von Baden (Gr1), Grosser Preis der Badischen Wirtschaft (Gr2), 3rd 126th Longines Grosser Preis von Berlin (Gr1), Grosser Preis der Badischen Wirtschaft (Gr2), www.pferdwetten.de - Grosser Hansa-Preis (Gr2), Preis von Dahlwitz (L)
Other stallions by his sire include: Sea The Stars (Gr1), Confuchias (winners), Halicarnassus (winners), Moohaajim (winners), Recharge (winners), Jet Away (3yo in 2019), Golden Horn (2yo), Awtaad (yearlings), Karpino (foals)

GUIGNOL (GER)

Cape Cross (IRE)	Green Desert (USA)	Danzig (USA)
		Foreign Courier (USA)
	Park Appeal	Ahonoora
		Balidaress
Guadalupe (GER)	Monsun (GER)	Konigsstuhl (GER)
		Mosella (GER)
	Guernica (GB)	Unfuwain (USA)
		Greenvera (USA)

MEKHTAAL (GB)

Three sons of Gilltown Stud's Timeform 140-rated champion Sea The Stars (by Cape Cross) are beginning their stallion careers in France in 2019: Chemical Charge, Cloth Of Stars, and Mekhtaal. The latter, who raced in the well-known Al Shaqab Racing colours, has joined the team at their Haras de Bouquetot and looks likely to be popular in his new role.

He was unraced at two, made a winning debut over 10 furlongs on heavy ground at Saint-Cloud in April of his three-year-old season, ran away with the Group 2 Prix Hocquart over the same distance on good ground at Deauville two months later, but then disappointed when only seventh to Almanzor in the Group 1 Prix du Jockey Club at Chantilly. He was a beaten favourite when fourth in the Group 1 Grand Prix de Paris a month later, and when a short-neck runner-up in the Group 3 Prix du Prince d'Orange at Maisons-Laffitte two months later, but got his top-level success the following season. He kicked off that campaign with a neck second to Cloth Of Stars in the Group 2 Prix d'Harcourt over 10 furlongs on good at Chantilly in early April and then landed the nine-furlong Group 1 Prix d'Ispahan at Chantilly, beating Robin Of Navan by a neck and with the high-class mare Usherette a half-length back in third.

Three unplaced runs in top-level company on faster ground followed, but he returned to training as a five-year-old, now with the powerful Graham Motion in North America, having previously been with Jean-Claude Rouget. He was a runner-up in both of his starts of 2018, beaten just half-length each time in 12-furlong contests at Woodbine in Canada. He was giving Tiz A Slam 2lbs when losing out to that colt in the Grade 2 Nijinsky Stakes in July, with Johnny Bear a neck back in third, and then lost out to that latter rival in the Grade 1 Northern Dancer Turf Stakes in mid-September.

Mekhtaal, who was Timeform-rated 115 at three and 120 at four, is out of the Group 3 Prix Fille de l'Air winner Aiglonne (by Silver Hawk) and that makes him a half-brother to Group

2 Prix Hocquart scorer Democrate (by Dalakhani) and to Aigue Marine (by Galileo) who won a pair of Grade 3 handicaps in the USA. His dam's siblings include Gaily Tiara (by Caerleon), the dam of Group 1 Prix Saint-Alary star and Group 1 Prix de Diane (French Oaks) runner-up Germance (by Silver Hawk), and that classic filly could be described as being Aiglonne's three-parts sister. Gaily Tiara is also the dam of the dual middle-distance French listed winner Gaily Game (by Montjeu).

Majestic Role (by Theatrical), the grandam of Mekhtaal, won the Listed Tyros Stakes in Ireland as a juvenile and was runner-up in the Group 1 Prix de la Salamandre, whereas her half-sister Fair Of The Furze (by Ela-Mana-Mou) got her best win in the Group 2 Tattersalls Gold Cup over 10 and a half furlongs at the Curragh before going on to a notable career as a broodmare. That one's son Fair Question (by Rainbow Quest) was a Group 2 scorer over 14 furlongs in Germany, her best daughter was listed scorer Elfaslah (by Green Desert) – dam of Group 1 Dubai World Cup winner and blacktype sire Almutawakel (by Machiavellian) – but her standout representative was White Muzzle (by Dancing Brave).

He won the Group 1 Derby Italiano, he was twice runner-up in the Group 1 King George VI and Queen Elizabeth Stakes at Ascot – to Opera House and to King's Theatre – and he was a neck runner-up to Urban Sea in the Group 1 Prix de l'Arc de Triomphe. He enjoyed some success at stud in Japan, his best offspring included Grade 1 Kikuka Sho (St Leger) winner and Grade 1 Tokyo Yushun (Derby) runner-up Asakusa Kings, and Grade 1 Japan Cup Dirt scorer Nihonpiro Ours, and he died in 2017, aged 27. Almutawakel, on the other hand, was only 12 when he died, but his offspring included Group 1 New Zealand Derby winner Wahid and Group 1 Derby Italiano scorer Awelmarduk.

This combination of pedigree and race record makes Mekhtaal an interesting addition to the stallion ranks. Some of his offspring will win at two, likely over seven furlongs and upwards, but his best results are likely to come with three-year-olds and older horses, mostly in the 10-15 furlong range.

SUMMARY DETAILS

Standing: Haras de Bouquetot
Fee: €5,000
Career highlights: 3 wins inc Prix d'Ispahan (Gr1), Prix
Hocquart (Gr2), 2nd Northern Dancer Turf Stakes (Gr1), Prix
d'Harcourt (Gr2), Nijinsky Stakes (Gr2), Prix du Prince
d'Orange (Gr3)
Other stallions by his sire include: Sea The Moon (Gr3),
Affinisea (yearlings in 2019), Harzand (yearlings), Storm The
Stars (foals), Zelzal (foals)

MEKHTAAL (GB) – chestnut 2013

Sea The Stars (IRE)	Cape Cross (IRE)	Green Desert (USA)
		Park Appeal
	Urban Sea (USA)	Miswaki (USA)
		Allegretta
Aiglonne (USA)	Silver Hawk (USA)	Roberto (USA)
		Gris Vitesse (USA)
	Majestic Role (FR)	Theatrical
		Autocratic

MR OWEN (USA)

It is a bit early yet to think of Invincible Spirit (by Green Desert) as a sire of sires – a term that used to be reserved for those who have at least five or six sons who have got Group 1 winners – but he can indeed be called a prolific sire of stallions. He is represented by one of the outstanding sires in Australia – I Am Invincible – as well as European classic sire Lawman and several others who have sired stakes winners. Some of those are very young, so still in the early stages of their career, and the potential standouts among them are last year's freshmen Charm Spirit and Kingman. Both were themselves brilliant milers, both got pattern winners among a double-digit tally of juvenile scorers, and at this point, it is Kingman who has shown the greater potential. That said, both look like becoming future Group 1 sires.

The list of Invincible Spirits who have not yet had runners includes 2019 freshman sire Cable Bay – who is related to the multiple New Zealand champion sire Volksraad – plus two-year-old star Shalaa and classic-placed miler Terrorities, both of whom have yearlings. Those whose first foals are arriving this year include juvenile Group 1 scorer National Defense, and Group 1 sprint star Profitable.

Mr Owen was not quite in their league as a racehorse, but he was a stakes winner at three, four, and five years of age, he was Group 3-placed at six, and the pick of his other form includes third to Make Believe in the Group 1 Poule d'Essai des Poulains (French 2000 Guineas). He was effective from seven to 10 furlongs, won on soft, very soft and good ground, and got two of his stakes wins on Polytrack at Deauville.

As his dam won the Group 1 Prix Vermeille over 12 furlongs and the Grade 1 E P Taylor Stakes over 10, it may seem that he got all of his speed from his sire. Invincible Spirit played a big part in that. However, Mrs Lindsay (by Theatrical) is a half-sister to Dame Dorothy (by Bernardini), who won the Grade 1 Humana Distaff Stakes over seven furlongs on dirt at Churchill Downs and a Grade 3 over eight and a half, so that hints at the mile to 10-furlong trend that is present in the family's past.

They are out of Vole Vole Monamour (by Woodman), who dead-heated in a 10-furlong contest on very soft ground at Chantilly as a three-year-old, but she, in turn, is a daughter of A Votre Sante (by Irish River), a six-length winner of the Listed Prix Camargo over a mile on good ground at Saint-Cloud before finishing a two-and-a-half-length fourth to Ta Rib in the Group 1 Poule d'Essai des Pouliches (French 1000 Guineas). Unaccounted For (by Private Account), the star half-brother to that mare, was placed in the Grade 1 Breeders' Cup Classic and Grade 1 Jockey Club Gold Cup over 10 but got his best wins in the Grade 1 Whitney Handicap and Grade 2 Jim Dandy Stakes, over nine.

That talented pair were the only foals out of dual juvenile listed scorer Mrs Jenney (by The Minstrel), and she, as her name might suggest, was a daughter of the excellent Mrs Penny (by Great Nephew). That star was England's champion juvenile filly of 1979 after wins in the Group 3 Cherry Hinton Stakes, Group 3 Lowther Stakes and Group 1 Cheveley Park Stakes. She was the champion again at three after a Timeform 127-rated season that saw her take the Group 1 Prix de Diane (French Oaks) and Group 1 Prix Vermeille, chase home Ela-Mana-Mou in the Group 1 King George VI and Queen Elizabeth Stakes, and pick up third place in both the Group 1 1000 Guineas and Group 1 Irish 1000 Guineas. Her pattern-placed stakes-winning son Northern Park had the distinction of being the final Northern Dancer (by Nearctic) yearling to be offered for sale – he made $2.8 million.

He did not achieve much at stud, but Mrs Penny's half-sister Cadeaux d'Amie (by Lyphard) became a broodmare of note. She had been placed in the Group 3 Prix d'Aumale and Group 3 Prix Vanteaux in her racing days, but her gelded son Irish Prize (by Irish River) was a Grade 1-winning miler in the USA and a full-brother to 1994 US Champion Turf Mare Hatoof. Despite her title, she was trained by Criquette Head in France, she won the Group 1 1000 Guineas and Group 1 Champion Stakes in England, landed the Grade 2 E P Taylor

Stakes in Canada, and the Group 2 Prix de l'Opera in France. Her US form featured victory in the Grade 1 Beverly D Stakes and a second-place finish to Tikkanen in the Grade 1 Breeders' Cup Turf. Her peak end-of-season Timeform rating was 124. Cadeaux d'Amie's descendants also include ill-fated Group 1 Irish Derby winner Trading Leather (by Teofilo) and Oaks-placed 10-furlong pattern scorer Pictavia (by Sinndar).

Mr Owen is not one of the more high-profile horses taking up stallion duties in 2019, but there is no doubt that he is well-bred, and it will be interesting to see what sort of support he receives. His best flat horses are, like him, likely to show their best in the seven-to-10-furlong range, with some staying a bit farther.

SUMMARY DETAILS

Standing: Haras du Petit Tellier
Fee: €3,000
Career highlights: 5 wins inc Prix de Tourgeville (L), Prix Lyphard (L), Prix Luthier (L), 2nd Prix Messidor (Gr3), Betway Winter Derby Stakes (Gr3), 3rd Poule d'Essai des Poulains (Gr1), Prix du Muguet (Gr2), British Stallion Studs EBF Hyde Stakes (L)
Other stallions by his sire include: I Am Invincible (Gr1), Lawman (Gr1), Kingman (Gr2), Zebedee (Gr2), Born To Sea (Gr3), Charm Spirit (Gr3), Vale Of York (Gr3), Captain Marvelous (L), Mayson (L), Swiss Spirit (winners), Cable Bay (2yo in 2019), Ajaya (yearlings), Life Force (yearlings), Shalaa (yearlings), Territories (yearlings), National Defense (foals), Profitable (foals), Shaiban (foals)

MR OWEN (USA) - bay 2012

Invincible Spirit (IRE)	Green Desert (USA)	Danzig (USA)
		Foreign Courier (USA)
	Rafha	Kris
		Eljazzi
Mrs Lindsay (USA)	Theatrical	Nureyev
		Tree Of Knowledge
	Vole Vole Monamour (USA)	Woodman (USA)
		A Votre Sante (USA)

RECOLETOS (FR)

Multiple Group 1 star Whipper (by Miesque's Son) looked full of promise when he retired to stud, and not just because of his considerable talent as a racehorse. He is by a full-brother to leading sire Kingmambo (by Mr Prospector), he could be described as being a three-parts brother to the top-class filly Divine Proportions (by Kingmambo), and his grandam was a full-sister to dual Derby hero and influential stallion Shirley Heights (by Mill Reef). He has three top-level winners among a total of 26 blacktype scorers, but that is from 10 crops of racing age, which is below the level of achievement that would have hoped of him.

He spent five years at Ballylinch Stud in Ireland, then five at Haras du Mezeray, two at Haras de Gelos, and he moved to Haras de Treban in 2018. His best before that year were Group 1 Prix d l'Abbaye de Longchamp heroine Wizz Kid, Italian mile Group 1 scorer Waikika, and the Group 1-placed Group 2 winners Pollyana, Royal Bench, and Recoletos. The latter took both the Group 2 Prix Greffulhe and Group 3 Prix du Prince d'Orange in 2017, finished third to Brametot in the Group 1 Prix du Jockey Club (French Derby), and fourth to Cracksman in the Group 1 Qipco Champion Stakes. Timeform rated him 118.

In 2018, Recoletos became a dual Group 1 winner, and the Timeform 125-rated star is now embarking on a stallion career of his own, at the famous Haras du Quesnay. He kicked off the season with a near two-length defeat of Jimmy Two Times in the Group 2 Prix du Muguet over a mile at Saint-Cloud and followed that with victory in the Group 1 Prix d'Ispahan at ParisLongchamp, this time beating Almodovar by a length and three-quarters. He disappointed when finishing only seventh behind Accidental Agent in the Group 1 Queen Anne Stakes at Royal Ascot in June, but bounced back from that to chase home Alpha Centauri in the Group 1 Prix du Haras de Fresney-le-Buffard Jacques le Marois at Deauville in August.

He then grabbed a second top-level win when getting up almost on the line to beat Wind Chimes by a head in the Group 1 Prix du Moulin de Longchamp – in which Expert Eye was another length and a half back in third – before heading to Ascot for what would be his final race. He was beaten just under two lengths when fifth to Roaring Lion in the Group 1 Queen Elizabeth II Stakes. Although both his pattern wins of 2017, plus his first one of 2018 came on soft ground, his second top-level victory came on good, so plenty of ease in the underfoot conditions was not a requisite for him. That said, the one time that he ran on fast ground resulted in the disappointing seventh-place finish at Royal Ascot.

Sarl Darpat France's homebred Recoletos stays farther than his sire did, but as he comes from the direct family of a Timeform 135-rated dual Derby hero, that's not a surprise. He is trained by Carlos Laffon-Parias, and he is the best of several winners for his dam, Highphar (by Highest Honor). His half-sister and stablemate Castellar (by American Post) won both the Group 2 Shadwell Prix de la Nonette and Group 3 Prix Cleopatre in 2018, and his dam is an unraced daughter of the Grade 2 Garden City Breeders' Cup Handicap and Group 3 Prix de Sandringham scorer Pharatta (by Fairy King). That talented filly, whose top wins came over nine and eight furlongs respectively, is out of the unraced Sharata (by Darshaan), which makes her a half-sister to Group 2 Premio Ribot and Group 3 September Stakes scorer Crimson Tide (by Sadler's Wells), a successful sire in Brazil.

The next dam is triple winner Shademah (by Thatch) and so Sharata, the third dam of Recoletos, is a half-sister to the Aga Khan's homebred dual Derby hero but poor stallion Shahrastani (by Nijinsky). He won the Group 3 Guardian Classic Trial and Group 2 Dante Stakes before that somewhat fortunate defeat of Dancing Brave at Epsom. Then he ran away with the Group 1 Irish Derby before finishing fourth behind his old rival in both the Group 1 King George VI and Queen Elizabeth Stakes at Ascot and Group 1 Prix de l'Arc de Triomphe at Longchamp in what was a vintage year – 1986.

His dam was a half-sister to Group 1 Grand Prix de Saint-Cloud winner Shakapour (by Kalamoun), Grade 1 Bowling Green Handicap scorer Sharannpour (by Busted), and Shashna (by Blakeney) – the unplaced dam of Group 1 Prix de Diane (French Oaks) heroine Shemaka (by Nishapour). They were out of Shamim (by Le Haar), a winning half-sister to the classic-placed Group 2 Prix du Conseil de Paris winner Kamaraan (by Tanerko).

Recoletos is not in the same league as his most famous relation – but then, few horses are. He is a classic-placed dual Group 1 winner, and although his best form came as a four-year-old, it is possible that this is at least in part due to him dropping down in distance this year rather than being entirely about maturity. He is to stand at one of France's most famous studs, and it would be no surprise to see him become a successful sire.

SUMMARY DETAILS

Standing: Haras du Quesnay
Fee: €8,000
Career highlights: 7 wins inc Prix du Moulin de Longchamp (Gr1), Churchill Coolmore Prix d'Ispahan (Gr1), Prix du Muguet (Gr2), Prix Greffulhe (Gr2), Prix du Prince d'Orange (Gr3), 2nd Prix du Haras de Fresney-le-Buffard Jacques le Marois (Gr1), 3rd Qipco Prix du Jockey Club (Gr1
Other stallions by his sire include: Very Nice Name (3yo in 2019)

RECOLETOS (FR) – bay 2014

Whipper (USA)	Miesque's Son (USA)	Mr Prospector (USA)
		Miesque (USA)
	Myth To Reality (FR)	Sadler's Wells (USA)
		Millieme
Highphar (FR)	Highest Honor (FR)	Kenmare (FR)
		High River (FR)
	Pharatta (IRE)	Fairy King (USA)
		Sharata (IRE)

SEABHAC (USA)

Seabhac had an unusual career in that he opened his winning account with a half-length score in the Grade 3 Pilgrim Stakes over eight and a half furlongs on turf at Belmont Park, and this came a month after he finished fourth to Catholic Boy in the Grade 3 With Anticipation Stakes over the same trip at Saratoga. He did not run again. His career lasted just three starts. However, he is a son of the late and much lamented Scat Daddy (by Johannesburg), so it is no surprise that he was snapped up for stallion duties. That new home is in France.

It is early days yet for the Scat Daddys at stud – he was only 11 when he died – but Daddy Long Legs created such an impression with his first crop in Chile that he was moved to Kentucky for 2019, and Coolmore Stud-based No Nay Never had his fee quadrupled, to €100,000, after a freshman year that yielded a string of stakes winners, led by Group 1 Juddmonte Middle Park Stakes star Ten Sovereigns.

Seabhac is out of the once-raced Curlin Hawk (by Curlin), a mare who has only three winners among 11 siblings. Each of that trio is a blacktype horse, one of them is the Grade 2-placed stakes-winning sprinter-miler Unforgettable Max (by Northern Afleet) and another is his champion and dual classic-winning full-brother Afleet Alex. That star took the Grade 2 Sanford Stakes and Grade 1 Hopeful Stakes at two, he added the Grade 2 Arkansas Derby, Grade 1 Preakness Stakes and Grade 1 Belmont Stakes at three, and he was third in the Grade 1 Kentucky Derby. He has also been successful at stud as his tally of more than 30 stakes winners includes six who have won at least once at the highest level.

Those two have a talented three-parts sister named Cash's Girl (by Northern Afleet) and her six wins, from five and a half to eight and a half furlongs, include four listed contests. She was Grade 3 placed, missed out on a Grade 1 placing when only fourth in the Matron Stakes, and she is the dam of last year's Grade 3 Monmouth Cup scorer Name Changer (by Uncle Mo). That prolific colt has won eight of his 17 starts, earned almost $500,000, won two listed races, been Grade 2-placed, and those bits of blacktype all came over nine furlongs.

Maggy Hawk (by Hawkster), the grandam of Seabhac, got her only win as a two-year-old, and it was at that age that her dam, Qualique (by Hawaii) won the Grade 1 Demoiselle Stakes at Aqueduct. That star also produced a low number of winners to foals born, but one of her successful three was Cue The Groom (by Blushing Groom), the dam of Italian Group 3 scorer and Group 1 Oaks d'Italia third Vale Mantovani (by Wolfhound), the dam of Group 1-placed multiple Italian stakes winner Duca Di Mantova (by Manduro).

Being a juvenile mile Grade 3 scorer by Scat Daddy and out of a half-sister to Afleet Alex makes Seabhac an interesting addition to the European stallion ranks. His pedigree suggests that he was going to be one of the quite typical US runners by his sire – a mile-to-10-furlong horse – rather than the sprinter type usually associated with him in Europe, and so it is likely that his two-year-olds, like himself, will be autumn and late-season ones, with his best results coming with three-year-olds and older horses, at seven furlongs and upwards.

SUMMARY DETAILS

Standing: Haras de Saint Arnoult
Fee: €5,000
Career highlights: 1 win inc Pilgrim Stakes (Gr3)
Other stallions by his sire include: Daddy Long Legs (Gr1), No Nay Never (Gr1), Daddy Nose Best (winners), Handsome Mike (winners), Frac Daddy (2yo of 2019), Caravaggio (foals), El Kabeir (foals)

SEABHAC (USA) – bay/brown 2015

Scat Daddy (USA)	Johannesburg (USA)	Hennessy (USA)
		Myth (USA)
	Love Style (USA)	Mr Prospector (USA)
		Likeable Style (USA)
Curlin Hawk (USA)	Curlin (USA)	Smart Strike (CAN)
		Sheriff's Deputy (USA)
	Maggy Hawk (USA)	Hawkster (USA)
		Qualique (USA)

SEAHENGE (USA)

Late Ashford Stud stallion Scat Daddy (by Johannesburg) has been all the rage these past few years, and the Coolmore team are among those who bought some of his high-priced colts. The rush is on to find the horse(s) who will carry on his male line.

They include an Aidan O'Brien-trained bay for whom they paid $750,000 at the Keeneland September Yearling Sale, but who will start his stallion career in France. Seahenge made a narrow winning debut over six furlongs at Naas in early July of his juvenile season and was then pitched straight into pattern company. His first attempt was disappointing – he was beaten by a total of eight lengths when finishing fifth behind Expert Eye in the Group 2 Qatar Vintage Stakes over seven at Goodwood – but then put up two better performances. He came from last to first to wear down Hey Gaman in the Group 2 Howcroft Industrial Supplies Champagne Stakes over the same trip at Doncaster, getting to the front near the line to score by a neck. Then he finished a five-length third to his stable companions U S Navy Flag and Mendelssohn in the Group 1 Darley Dewhurst Stakes at Newmarket.

This first season suggested that he could be a potential classic colt in the making, but not only did he fail to win again, but he made the frame once from five starts, all of them as a three-year-old. That bit of blacktype came when finishing a four-and-a-half-length third to Mendelssohn in the Listed 32Red Patton Stakes over a mile at Dundalk in March. He was a well-beaten fifth in the Grade 2 UAE Derby at Meydan then well beaten in a pair of Grade 3 one-mile contests in the USA and, on his final start, in the Grade 1 Sword Dancer Stakes over 12 furlongs at Saratoga.

He is one of four sons of Scat Daddy who have taken up a stallion position in Europe in 2019, and the others are Seabhac, Sioux Nation, and Smooth Daddy. The first few of his sons with runners include two who made such a notable start with their first crop that they were rewarded with a significant change in their status. Daddy Long Legs was champion freshman sire in Chile and got a Grade 1 star in his first crop, and he is now in Kentucky. No Nay Never, on the other hand, got a string of stakes-winning juveniles in his first crop in 2018, headed by the unbeaten Group 1 Middle Park Stakes star Ten Sovereigns, and Coolmore quadrupled his fee for 2019. At €100,000, the quality of mares that he receives will soar compared to the support he got before.

The new Scat Daddy stallions in the USA this year are headed by the Grade 1 standouts Mendelssohn and Justify. The former is a half-brother to champion mare Beholder (by Henny Hughes) and, more importantly concerning his sire potential, is a half-brother to leading US sire Into Mischief (by Harlan's Holiday). Justify, of course, is the first US Triple Crown hero to retire to stud undefeated. Both stand at Coolmore's Ashford Stud in Kentucky.

Seahenge is the best of three blacktype earners out of listed scorer Fools In Love (by Not For Love), who won at up to eight and a half furlongs. The mare is among a string of winners out of triple scorer Parlez (by French Deputy), which makes her a full-sister to a high-earning listed race winner and half-sister to Grade 2 Louisiana Derby and Grade 2 Risen Star Stakes winner International Star (by Fusaichi Pegasus), and her grandam is Speak Halory (by Verbatim), a stakes-placed half-sister to several horses of note.

Halory Hunter (by Jade Hunter) won the Grade 2 Blue Grass Stakes, finished third in the Grade 1 Florida Derby and fourth in the Grade 1 Kentucky Derby, whereas $6.4 million yearling and former Ballydoyle-based trainee Van Nistelrooy (by Storm Cat) took the Group 2 Futurity Stakes, was runner-up in the Group 1 National Stakes and third in the Group 2 Royal Lodge Stakes before going on to some success at stud. He is bred on similar lines to Seahenge, and his roll of honour features a Grade 1 scorer in Argentina and a middle-distance classic star in New Zealand. Halory Hunter also sired some blacktype horses though nothing of real note.

Their siblings Brushed Halory, Key Lory and Prory all won at Grade 3 level, and their one-time successful half-sister Miss

Halory did her part for the family by coming up with the ill-fated eight and a half-furlong Grade 3 scorer Stormalory (by Storm Cat). There are various other stakes winners under the first four generations of the family, including Group 3 Jebel Ali Mile scorer Shamaal Nibras (by First Samurai) and Group 2 Prix Eugene Adam winner Gyllen (by Medaglia d'Oro).

As a Group 1-placed juvenile Group 2 winner, Seahenge showed ability and precocity. He is inbred 5x3x3 to Mr Prospector (by Raise a Native), is a smart seven-furlong horse who was bred to be a high-class miler, and so it will be interesting to see how he gets on in his new career. He should be capable of getting winners in all age groups, and depending on the mares, his best could be most effective at anywhere from five to 10 furlongs.

SUMMARY DETAILS

Standing: Haras de la Haie Neuve
Fee: €5,000
Career highlights: 2 wins inc Howcroft Champagne Stakes (Gr2), 3rd Darley Dewhurst Stakes (Gr1), 32Red Patton Stakes (L)
Other stallions by his sire include: Daddy Long Legs (Gr1), No Nay Never (Gr1), Daddy Nose Best (winners), Handsome Mike (winners), Frac Daddy (2yo of 2019), Caravaggio (foals), El Kabeir (foals)

SEAHENGE (USA) – bay 2015

Scat Daddy (USA)	Johannesburg (USA)	Hennessy (USA)
		Myth (USA)
	Love Style (USA)	**Mr Prospector (USA)**
		Likeable Style (USA)
Fools In Love (USA)	Not For Love (USA)	**Mr Prospector (USA)**
		Dance Number (USA)
	Parlez (USA)	French Deputy (USA)
		Speak Halory (USA)

SUMBAL (IRE)

Sumbal began his career in good style with a trio of easy wins that culminated in a six-length score on very soft ground in the Group 2 Prix Greffulhe. However, he could finish only fifth to New Bay in the Group 1 Prix du Jockey Club (French Derby), and the best he managed subsequently was a trio of pattern-race placings, also over 10 furlongs.

His late sire was a dual Group 1 winner at two, he was a leading shuttle sire, and his 172 stakes winners featured 22 who won at the highest level. Danehill Dancer (by Danehill) also became a noted sire of some good stallions, with Choisir and rising star Mastercraftsman the most successful. Fast Company has hit the Group 1 target in both hemispheres, Monsieur Bond supplies sprinters, whereas both Lizard Island and Silent Times made their name in South America.

Sumbal is out of Group 2 Prix du Conseil de Paris second Alix Road (by Linamix), and his siblings include two talented fillies. Lily Passion (by Sea The Stars) has won a listed race in France, and although Lavendar Lane (by Shamardal) is not a stakes winner, she has been placed in both the Group 2 Prix de Mallaret and Group 2 Prix de la Nonette, among other blacktype events. One of Alix Road's half-sisters produced the Group 3 Prix de la Nonette winner Viane Rose (by Sevres Rose), and she was out of Life On The Road (by Persian Heights), a half-sister to listed scorer West Side (by Tel Quel).

Arkova (by Irish River), the unraced third dam of Sumbal, was out of Group 2 Prix Maurice de Nieuil scorer Singapore Girl (by Lyphard) and so was a half-sister to 11 winners. The most notable of these was the talented middle-distance performer Gunboat Diplomacy (by Dominion), who won the Group 2 Prix Noailles, Group 3 Prix Exbury, Group 3 Prix des Chenes, and Group 3 La Coupe de Maisons-Laffitte, was runner-up in the Group 1 Prix d'Ispahan, and fourth in the Group 1 Prix Lupin. He sired 54 foals, and they included the Grade 2-winning chaser Kario De Sormain. Arvoka's siblings also include the dam of Argentine champion and triple Grade

1 star Riton (by Un Desperado) who is just one of the many blacktype winners who appear under various branches of the fourth generation of the family.

It remains to be seen what sort of support Sumbal will receive, but it seems likely that he will attract the attention of the National Hunt sector, especially given his relationship to Gunboat Diplomacy.

SUMMARY DETAILS

Standing: Haras de Grandcamp

Fee: €3,000

Career highlights: 3 wins inc Prix Greffulhe (Gr2), 2nd Prix d'Harcourt (Gr2), Prix Exbury (Gr3), Prix du Prince d'Orange (Gr3)

Other stallions by his sire include: Air Chief Marshal (Gr1), Choisir (Gr1), Fast Company (Gr1), Lizard Island (Gr1), Mastercraftsman (Gr1), Monsieur Bond (Gr1), Silent Times (Gr1), Indesatchel (Gr2), Jeremy (Gr2), Alfred Nobel (Gr3), Planteur (L), Where Or When (L), Hillstar (2yo in 2019)

SUMBAL (IRE) – grey 2012

Danehill Dancer (IRE)	Danehill (USA)	Danzig (USA)
		Razyana (USA)
	Mira Adonde (USA)	Sharpen Up
		Lettre D'Amour (USA)
Alix Road (FR)	Linamix (FR)	Mendez (FR)
		Lunadix (FR)
	Life On The Road (IRE)	Persian Heights
		Arkova

TAAREEF (USA)

US Champion sire Kitten's Joy (by El Prado) has three notable sons who are beginning their stallion career in Europe in 2019: multiple Group 1 stars Hawkbill and Roaring Lion, and high-class Taareef. The first two are in England, but the dual Group 2 Qatar Prix Daniel Wildenstein winner is in France. His seven wins from 15 starts also included a trio of Group 3 contests, the races in which he was placed featured a three-quarter-length second to Ribchester in the Group 1 Qatar Prix du Moulin de Longchamp, and he was only out of the first four twice.

Hawkbill got his best wins at 10 and 12 furlongs, Roaring Lion was placed in the Derby, and his class got him through in the one-mile Queen Elizabeth II Stakes, but he was best at 10 furlongs. Taareef, on the other hand, was only fourth to Almanzor in the Group 2 Prix Guillaume d'Ornano on his sole attempt at 10 furlongs, he was a pattern winner and a fourth-place finisher in two tries at nine furlongs, but entirely at home over a mile.

He is the best of several winners out of the stakes-placed five-time scorer Sacred Feather (by Carson City), a mare who has five stakes-winning siblings. They include the Grade 3 scorers Christine's Outlaw (by Wild Again) and Marastani (by Shahrastani), the former best at eight and nine furlongs, and the latter a gelding whose best win came over 12 furlongs on turf. Their half-sister Smile N Molly (by Dixieland Band) had no blacktype, but this two-time winner was the dam of Don't Tell The Kids (by Carson City) and the best of his 10 wins came in the Grade 3 Sapling Stakes over six furlongs on dirt as a two-year-old. He could be described as being a three-parts brother to Taareef's dam.

Grade 3 scorer Marianna's Girl (by Dewan), the grandam of Haras de Mezeray's new horse, was effective at around a mile and the best of her siblings was Bold Style (by Bold Commander). He won the Grade 2 Oaklawn Handicap when it was run over eight and a half furlongs, plus the Grade 3

Inglewood Handicap over the same trip, and the races in which he was placed included the Grade 1 Whitney Handicap and Grade 1 Arkansas Derby, both over nine. His Grade 3-placed, stakes-winning half-brother Set Free (by Majestic Prince) sired a handful of blacktype earners and multiple winners from limited opportunities.

There are quite a few other stakes winners to be found under branches of the third generation of the pedigree, and if you go back another step, then you will see that third dam Marianna Trench (by Pago Pago). She won three times, was a half-sister to eight-and-a-half-furlong Grade 3 scorer Go Honey Go (by General Assembly) – dam of Japanese blacktype-winning sprinter Gaily Flash (by Danehill) – and The Caretaker (by Caerleon), whom Irish racegoers may remember. She won the Listed Silver Flash Stakes and the Cartier Million at two, she added the Listed Knockaire Stakes and Listed Derrinstown Stud 1000 Guineas Trial at three, and was later blacktype-placed in the USA before going on to a notable broodmare career.

Her star daughter was the Dermot Weld-trained Dimitrova (by Swain) who was a Leopardstown listed winner and Group 1 Irish 1000 Guineas third before adding the Grade 1 Flower Bowl Invitational Stakes over 10 furlongs at Belmont Park. The Caretaker's top son was Mutafaweq (by Silver Hawk), the Group 1 St Leger hero of 1999. He also won the Group 1 Coronation Cup, Group 1 Deutschland Preis, and Grade 1 Canadian International Stakes. His offspring include the Group 1-placed Japanese miler Meiner Falke.

Taareef, who cost $675,000 at the Keeneland September Yearling Sale, represents a cross between the Sadler's Wells (by Northern Dancer) and Mr Prospector (by Raise a Native) sire lines. He was a high-class miler who won his only two starts as a juvenile and who earned a peak end-of-season Timeform rating of 125. He is a promising new addition to the stallion ranks and looks likely to get his best in the seven-to-12-furlong range.

SUMMARY DETAILS

Standing: Haras du Mezeray

Fee: €6,000

Career highlights: 7 wins inc Qatar Prix Daniel Wildenstein (Gr2-twice), Prix Daphnis (Gr3), Prix Bertrand du Breuil Longines (Gr3), Prix Messidor (Gr3), 2nd Qatar Prix du Moulin de Longchamp (Gr1), Prix de Fontainebleau (Gr3), 3rd Prix du Muguet (Gr2)

Other stallions by his sire include: Real Solution (winners), Big Blue Kitten (yearlings), Bobby's Kitten (yearlings)

TAAREEF (USA) – chestnut 2013

Kitten's Joy (USA)	El Prado (IRE)	Sadler's Wells (USA)
		Lady Capulet (USA)
	Kitten's First (USA)	Lear Fan (USA)
		That's My Hon (USA)
Sacred Feather (USA)	Carson City (USA)	Mr Prospector (USA)
		Blushing Promise (USA)
	Marianna's Girl (USA)	Dewan (USA)
		Marianna Trench (USA)

TUNIS (POL)

Are you a fan of the Guillaume Macaire-trained Master Dino? Throughout his career to date he has had quite a rivalry with his Polish-bred stablemate Tunis, each winning several of their encounters. The gelding, who had looked a likely 2019 Cheltenham Festival contender, is currently on the sidelines due to an injury picked up following an easy victory at Plumpton in early January, but even when he makes it back to the track, he won't be facing his old foe again.

Tunis, who represents the first crop of Estejo (by Johan Cruyff) – a grandson of Danehill (by Danzig) who won the Group 1 Group 1 Premio Presidente della Repubblica and Group 1 Premio Roma – has taken up stallion duties in France. They are both just five years old, so perhaps Master Dino will eventually have the chance to race against some of Tunis's offspring. The new recruit has been a multiple graded winner over hurdles at Auteuil, chased home Master Dino in the Grade 1 Prix Renaud du Vivier - Grande Course de Haies des 4 Ans (Hurdle) over two miles, three and a half furlongs at that venue in November, and he is a fascinating addition to the stallion ranks.

He also ran twice on the flat as a two-year-old – finishing third and winning a mile contest at Warsaw – his dam won over six furlongs, and her other flat runners include winners over six, seven and eight furlongs in Poland. The mare's name is Tracja and she is a daughter of Llandaff (by Lyphard), the high-class son of outstanding middle-distance filly Dahlia (by Vaguely Noble), the Timeform 135-rated champion who went on to become one of the greatest broodmares of all time, with five top-level winners to her name plus two Group 2 scorers.

His grandam won at two, his third dam won nine times, and his fourth dam's two multiple winners – from just three foals – include the dam of the horse who won the Polish St Leger in 1996. There is nothing on the page to suggest why Tunis became such a good hurdler, but his race record makes him look like an ideal candidate to achieve success as a

National Hunt stallion in France, a country where leading sires of jumpers are often horses who themselves showed talent over hurdles, or even over fences.

SUMMARY DETAILS

Standing: Haras de Cercy

Fee: €3,000

Career highlights: 6 wins inc Prix Amadou (NH-2), Prix d'Indy (NH-3), Prix Aguado (NH-3), Prix Stanley (NH-L), 2nd Prix Renaud du Vivier - Grande Course de Haies des 4 Ans (NH-1), Prix Cambaceres - Grande Course de Haies des 3 Ans (NH-1), Prix Georges de Talhouet-Roy Royal Palm Beachcomer (NH-2), Prix de Maisons-Laffitte (NH-3), Prix Questarabad (NH-3), Prix Robert Lejeune (NH-L), 3rd Prix Pierre de Lassus (NH-3)

Other stallions by his sire include: none

TUNIS (POL)

Estejo (GER)	Johan Cruyff (GB)	Danehill (USA)
		Teslemi (USA)
	Este (GER)	The Noble Player (USA)
		Ermione
Tracja (POL)	Llandaff (USA)	Lyphard (USA)
		Dahlia (USA)
	Turbia (POL)	Nible
		Truskawka (POL)

NEW SIRES OF 2019
BY STUD

Ireland
Castlehyde Stud – Gustav Klimt (IRE)
Castlehyde Stud – Order Of St George (IRE)
Castlehyde Stud – Sioux Nation (USA)

Clongiffen Stud – Smooth Daddy (USA)

Coolmore Stud – Merchant Navy (AUS)
Coolmore Stud – Saxon Warrior (JPN)
Coolmore Stud – U S Navy Flag (USA)

Kildangan Stud – Jungle Cat (IRE)

Rathbarry Stud – James Garfield (IRE)

Tally-Ho Stud – Kessaar (IRE)

United Kingdom
Banstead Manor Stud – Expert Eye (GB)

Batsford Stud – Harbour Law (GB)

Bearstone Stud – Washington DC (IRE)

Cheveley Park Stud – Unfortunately (IRE)

Dalham Hall Stud – Cracksman (GB)
Dalham Hall Stud – Harry Angel (IRE)
Dalham Hall Stud – Hawkbill (USA)

GG Bloodstock and Racing – Master Carpenter (IRE)

Mickley Stud – Massaat (IRE)

National Stud – Lancaster Bomber (USA)
National Stud – Rajasinghe (IRE)

Nunnery Stud – Poet's Word (IRE)
Nunnery Stud – Tasleet (GB)

Tweenhills Farm & Stud – Lightning Spear (GB)
Tweenhills Farm & Stud – Roaring Lion (USA)
Tweenhills Farm & Stud – Zoustar (AUS)

Whitsbury Manor Stud – Havana Grey (GB)

Worsall Grange Stud – Dylan Mouth (IRE)

France
Haras d'Annebault – Guignol (GER)

Haras de Bouquetot – Mekhtaal (GB)

Haras de Cercy – Tunis (POL)

Haras de Grandcamp – Chemical Charge (IRE)
Haras de Grandcamp – Sumbal (IRE)

Haras de la Barbottière – Chanducoq (FR)

Haras de la Haie Neuve – Seahenge (USA)

Haras de Saint Arnoult – Dschingis Secret (GER)
Haras de Saint Arnoult – Seabhac (USA)

Haras du Hoguenet – Doha Dream (FR)

Haras du Logis – Cloth Of Stars (IRE)

Haras du Mezeray – Taareef (USA)

Haras du Petit Tellier – Mr Owen (USA)

Haras du Quesnay – Recoletos (FR)

NEW SIRES OF 2019
BY SIRE

Acclamation (GB) – Expert Eye (GB)

Cape Cross (IRE) – Guignol (GER)

Choisir (AUS) – Rajasinghe (IRE)

Danehill Dancer (IRE) – Sumbal (IRE)

Dark Angel (IRE) – Harry Angel (IRE)

Deep Impact (JPN) – Saxon Warrior (JPN)

Dylan Thomas (IRE) – Dylan Mouth (IRE)

Estejo (GER) – Tunis (POL)

Exceed And Excel (AUS) – James Garfield (IRE)

Fastnet Rock (AUS) – Merchant Navy (AUS)

Frankel (GB) – Cracksman (GB)

Galileo (IRE) – Gustav Klimt (IRE)
Galileo (IRE) – Order Of St George (IRE)

Havana Gold (IRE) – Havana Grey (GB)

Iffraaj (GB) – Jungle Cat (IRE)

Invincible Spirit (IRE) – Mr Owen (USA)

BY SIRE

Kitten's Joy (USA) – Hawkbill (USA)
Kitten's Joy (USA) – Roaring Lion (USA)
Kitten's Joy (USA) – Taareef (USA)

Kodiac (GB) – Kessaar (IRE)

Lawman (FR) – Harbour Law (GB)

Mastercraftsman (IRE) – Master Carpenter (IRE)

Northern Meteor (AUS) – Zoustar (AUS)

Pivotal (GB) – Lightning Spear (GB)

Poet's Voice (GB) – Poet's Word (IRE)

Scat Daddy (USA) – Seabhac (USA)
Scat Daddy (USA) – Seahenge (USA)
Scat Daddy (USA) – Sioux Nation (USA)
Scat Daddy (USA) – Smooth Daddy (USA)

Sea The Stars (IRE) – Chemical Charge (IRE)
Sea The Stars (IRE) – Cloth Of Stars (IRE)
Sea The Stars (IRE) – Mekhtaal (GB)

Shamardal (USA) – Doha Dream (FR)

Showcasing (GB) – Tasleet (GB)

Society Rock (IRE) – Unfortunately (IRE)

Soldier Hollow (GB) – Dschingis Secret (GER)

Teofilo (IRE) – Massaat (IRE)

Voix Du Nord (FR) – Chanducoq (FR)

War Front (USA) – Lancaster Bomber (USA)
War Front (USA) – U S Navy Flag (USA)

Whipper (USA) – Recoletos (FR)

Zoffany (IRE) – Washington DC (IRE)

NEW SIRES OF 2019
BY GRANDSIRE

Acclamation (GB) – Harry Angel (IRE), by Dark Angel (IRE)

Cape Cross (IRE) – Chemical Charge (IRE), by Sea The Stars (IRE)
Cape Cross (IRE) – Cloth Of Stars (IRE), by Sea The Stars (IRE)
Cape Cross (IRE) – Mekhtaal (GB), by Sea The Stars (IRE)

Danehill (USA) – Dylan Mouth (IRE), by Dylan Thomas (IRE)
Danehill (USA) – James Garfield (IRE), by Exceed And Excel (AUS)
Danehill (USA) – Kessaar (IRE), by Kodiac (GB)
Danehill (USA) – Merchant Navy (AUS), by Fastnet Rock (AUS)
Danehill (USA) – Sumbal (IRE), by Danehill Dancer (IRE)

Danehill Dancer (IRE) – Master Carpenter (IRE), by Mastercraftsman (IRE)
Danehill Dancer (IRE) – Rajasinghe (IRE), by Choisir (AUS)

Dansili (GB) – Washington DC (IRE), by Zoffany (IRE)

Danzig (USA) – Lancaster Bomber (USA), by War Front (USA)
Danzig (USA) – U S Navy Flag (USA), by War Front (USA)

Dubawi (IRE) – Poet's Word (IRE), by Poet's Voice (GB)

El Prado (IRE) – Hawkbill (USA), by Kitten's Joy (USA)
El Prado (IRE) – Roaring Lion (USA), by Kitten's Joy (USA)
El Prado (IRE) – Taareef (USA), by Kitten's Joy (USA)

Encosta De Lago (AUS) – Zoustar (AUS), by Northern Meteor (AUS)

Galileo (IRE) – Cracksman (GB), by Frankel (GB)
Galileo (IRE) – Massaat (IRE), by Teofilo (IRE)

Giant's Causeway (USA) – Doha Dream (FR), by Shamardal (USA)

Green Desert (USA) – Guignol (GER), by Cape Cross (IRE)
Green Desert (USA) – Mr Owen (USA), by Invincible Spirit (IRE)

In The Wings – Dschingis Secret (GER), by Soldier Hollow (GB)

Invincible Spirit (IRE) – Harbour Law (GB), by Lawman (FR)

Johan Cruyff (GB) – Tunis (POL), by Estejo (GER)

Johannesburg (USA) – Seabhac (USA), by Scat Daddy (USA)
Johannesburg (USA) – Seahenge (USA), by Scat Daddy (USA)
Johannesburg (USA) – Sioux Nation (USA), by Scat Daddy (USA)
Johannesburg (USA) – Smooth Daddy (USA), by Scat Daddy (USA)

Miesque's Son (USA) – Recoletos (FR), by Whipper (USA)

Oasis Dream (GB) – Tasleet (GB), by Showcasing (GB)

Polar Falcon (USA) – Lightning Spear (GB), by Pivotal (GB)

Rock Of Gibraltar (IRE) – Unfortunately (IRE), by Society Rock (IRE)

Royal Applause (GB) – Expert Eye (GB), by Acclamation (GB)

Sadler's Wells (USA) – Gustav Klimt (IRE), by Galileo (IRE)
Sadler's Wells (USA) – Order Of St George (IRE), by Galileo (IRE)

Sunday Silence (USA) – Saxon Warrior (JPN), by Deep Impact (JPN)

Teofilo (IRE) – Havana Grey (GB), by Havana Gold (IRE)

Valanour (IRE) – Chanducoq (FR), by Voix Du Nord (FR)

Zafonic (USA) – Jungle Cat (IRE), by Iffraaj (GB)

NEW SIRES OF 2019
BY GREAT-GRANDSIRE

Danehill (USA) – Master Carpenter (IRE), by Mastercraftsman (IRE), by Danehill Dancer (IRE)

Danehill (USA) – Rajasinghe (IRE), by Choisir (AUS), by Danehill Dancer (IRE)

Danehill (USA) – Tunis (POL), by Estejo (GER), by Johan Cruyff (GB)

Danehill (USA) – Unfortunately (IRE), by Society Rock (IRE), by Rock Of Gibraltar (IRE)

Danehill (USA) – Washington DC (IRE), by Zoffany (IRE), by Dansili (GB)

Danzig (USA) – Dylan Mouth (IRE), by Dylan Thomas (IRE), by Danehill (USA)

Danzig (USA) – Guignol (GER), by Cape Cross (IRE), by Green Desert (USA)

Danzig (USA) – James Garfield (IRE), by Exceed And Excel (AUS), by Danehill (USA)

Danzig (USA) – Kessaar (IRE), by Kodiac (GB), by Danehill (USA)

Danzig (USA) – Merchant Navy (AUS), by Fastnet Rock (AUS), by Danehill (USA)

Danzig (USA) – Mr Owen (USA), by Invincible Spirit (IRE), by Green Desert (USA)

Danzig (USA) – Sumbal (IRE), by Danehill Dancer (IRE), by Danehill (USA)

Dubai Millennium (GB) – Poet's Word (IRE), by Poet's Voice (GB), by Dubawi (IRE)

Fairy King (USA) – Zoustar (AUS), by Northern Meteor (AUS), by Encosta De Lago (AUS)

Galileo (IRE) – Havana Grey (GB), by Havana Gold (IRE), by Teofilo (IRE)

Gone West (USA) – Jungle Cat (IRE), by Iffraaj (GB), by Zafonic (USA)

Green Desert (USA) – Chemical Charge (IRE), by Sea The Stars (IRE), by Cape Cross (IRE)
Green Desert (USA) – Cloth Of Stars (IRE), by Sea The Stars (IRE), by Cape Cross (IRE)
Green Desert (USA) – Harbour Law (GB), by Lawman (FR), by Invincible Spirit (IRE)
Green Desert (USA) – Mekhtaal (GB), by Sea The Stars (IRE), by Cape Cross (IRE)
Green Desert (USA) – Tasleet (GB), by Showcasing (GB), by Oasis Dream (GB)

Halo (USA) – Saxon Warrior (JPN), by Deep Impact (JPN), by Sunday Silence (USA)

Hennessy (USA) – Seabhac (USA), by Scat Daddy (USA), by Johannesburg (USA)
Hennessy (USA) – Seahenge (USA), by Scat Daddy (USA), by Johannesburg (USA)
Hennessy (USA) – Sioux Nation (USA), by Scat Daddy (USA), by Johannesburg (USA)
Hennessy (USA) – Smooth Daddy (USA), by Scat Daddy (USA), by Johannesburg (USA)

Lomond (USA) – Chanducoq (FR), by Voix Du Nord (FR), by
Valanour (IRE)

Mr Prospector (USA) – Recoletos (FR), by Whipper (USA), by
Miesque's Son (USA)

Northern Dancer (CAN) – Gustav Klimt (IRE), by Galileo (IRE),
by Sadler's Wells (USA)
Northern Dancer (CAN) – Lancaster Bomber (USA), by War
Front (USA), by Danzig (USA)
Northern Dancer (CAN) – Order Of St George (IRE), by Galileo
(IRE), by Sadler's Wells (USA)
Northern Dancer (CAN) – U S Navy Flag (USA), by War Front
(USA), by Danzig (USA)

Nureyev (USA) – Lightning Spear (GB), by Pivotal (GB), by Polar
Falcon (USA)

Royal Applause (GB) – Harry Angel (IRE), by Dark Angel (IRE),
by Acclamation (GB)

Sadler's Wells (USA) – Cracksman (GB), by Frankel (GB), by
Galileo (IRE)
Sadler's Wells (USA) – Dschingis Secret (GER), by Soldier
Hollow (GB), by In The Wings
Sadler's Wells (USA) – Hawkbill (USA), by Kitten's Joy (USA), by
El Prado (IRE)
Sadler's Wells (USA) – Massaat (IRE), by Teofilo (IRE), by
Galileo (IRE)
Sadler's Wells (USA) – Roaring Lion (USA), by Kitten's Joy
(USA), by El Prado (IRE)
Sadler's Wells (USA) – Taareef (USA), by Kitten's Joy (USA),
by El Prado (IRE)

Storm Cat (USA) – Doha Dream (FR), by Shamardal (USA), by Giant's Causeway (USA)

Waajib – Expert Eye (GB), by Acclamation (GB), by Royal Applause (GB)

NEW SIRES OF 2019
BY BROODMARE SIRE

Acclamation (GB) – Massaat (IRE), by Teofilo (IRE)

Badger Land (USA) – Smooth Daddy (USA), by Scat Daddy (USA)

Cadeaux Genereux – Harry Angel (IRE), by Dark Angel (IRE)
Cadeaux Genereux – Tasleet (GB), by Showcasing (GB)

Carson City (USA) – Taareef (USA), by Kitten's Joy (USA)

Curlin (USA) – Seabhac (USA), by Scat Daddy (USA)

Danehill (USA) – Gustav Klimt (IRE), by Galileo (IRE)

Dansili (GB) – Expert Eye (GB), by Acclamation (GB), by Royal Applause (GB)

Dark Angel (IRE) – Havana Grey (GB), by Havana Gold (IRE)

Daylami (IRE) – James Garfield (IRE), by Exceed And Excel (AUS)

Forest Wildcat (USA) – Jungle Cat (IRE), by Iffraaj (GB)

Galileo (IRE) – Saxon Warrior (JPN), by Deep Impact (JPN)
Galileo (IRE) – U S Navy Flag (USA), by War Front (USA)

Giant's Causeway (USA) – Hawkbill (USA), by Kitten's Joy (USA)

Gone West (USA) – Order Of St George (IRE), by Galileo (IRE)

Highest Honor (FR) – Recoletos (FR), by Whipper (USA)

In The Wings – Master Carpenter (IRE), by Mastercraftsman (IRE)

Indian Ridge – Lancaster Bomber (USA), by War Front (USA)

King's Best (USA) – Doha Dream (FR), by Shamardal (USA)

Kingmambo (USA) – Chemical Charge (IRE), by Sea The Stars (IRE)

Kingmambo (USA) – Cloth Of Stars (IRE), by Sea The Stars (IRE)

Komaite (USA) – Unfortunately (IRE), by Society Rock (IRE)

Linamix (FR) – Sumbal (IRE), by Danehill Dancer (IRE)

Llandaff (USA) – Tunis (POL), by Estejo (GER)

Monsun (GER) – Guignol (GER), by Cape Cross (IRE)

Nashwan (USA) – Poet's Word (IRE), by Poet's Voice (GB)

Nikos – Chanducoq (FR), by Voix Du Nord (FR)

Not For Love (USA) – Seahenge (USA), by Scat Daddy (USA)

Noverre (USA) – Dylan Mouth (IRE), by Dylan Thomas (IRE)

Oasis Dream (GB) – Sioux Nation (USA), by Scat Daddy (USA)

Pivotal (GB) – Cracksman (GB), by Frankel (GB)

175

NEW SIRES OF 2019

Pivotal (GB) – Harbour Law (GB), by Lawman (FR)

Platini (GER) – Dschingis Secret (GER), by Soldier Hollow (GB)

Raven's Pass (USA) – Kessaar (IRE), by Kodiac (GB)

Redoute's Choice (AUS) – Zoustar (AUS), by Northern Meteor (AUS)

Royal Academy (USA) – Lightning Spear (GB), by Pivotal (GB)

Shinko Forest (IRE) – Washington DC (IRE), by Zoffany (IRE)

Silver Hawk (USA) – Mekhtaal (GB), by Sea The Stars (IRE)

Snippets (AUS) – Merchant Navy (AUS), by Fastnet Rock (AUS)

Soviet Star (USA) – Rajasinghe (IRE), by Choisir (AUS)

Street Sense (USA) – Roaring Lion (USA), by Kitten's Joy (USA)

Theatrical – Mr Owen (USA), by Invincible Spirit (IRE)

NEW SIRES OF 2019
BY DATE OF EARLIEST WIN

February
22 - Smooth Daddy (USA) - 1m maiden special weight at Gulfsteam Park, USA - 3yo

March
02 - Merchant Navy (AUS) - 6f maiden on good at Pakenham, Australia - 2yo

09 - Recoletos (USA) - 11f maiden on very soft at Fontainebleau, France - 3yo

10 - Sumbal (IRE) - 10f newcomers on very soft at Saint-Cloud, France, 3yo

11 - Doha Dream (FR) - 11f maiden on very soft at Fontainebleau, France - 3yo

12 - Mekhtaal (GB) - 10f newcomers on heavy at Saint-Cloud, France - 3yo

15 - Mr Owen (USA) - 1m maiden on very soft at Saint-Cloud, France - 3yo

26 - Dschingis Secret (GER) - 11f on heavy ground at Dusseldorf, Germany - 3yo

April
05 - Master Carpenter (IRE) - 5f maiden on good-to-soft at Leicester, England - 2yo

17 - Zoustar (AUS) - 5.5f maiden at Canterbury Park, Australia - 2yo

19 - Guignol (GER) - 11f on good at Cologne, Germany - 3yo

23 - Washington DC (IRE) - 5f maiden on good at Tipperary, Ireland - 2yo

May

01 - Harbour Law (GB) - 12f maiden on good-to-soft at Salisbury, England - 3yo

06 - Poet's Word (IRE) - 10f maiden on good-to-firm at Nottingham, England - 3yo

08 - Havana Grey (GB) - 5f novice on good-to-firm at Ayr, Scotland - 2yo

19 - Rajasinghe (IRE) - 6f novice on standard at Newcastle, England - 2yo

19 - Sioux Nation (USA) - 6f maiden on good at Cork, Ireland - 2yo

19 - Unfortunately (IRE) - 5f novice on good-to-firm at Hamilton, Scotland - 2yo

June

06 - Jungle Cat (IRE) - 6f maiden on good at Goodwood, England - 2yo

15 - Expert Eye (GB) - 6.5f novice on good at Newbury, England - 2yo

30 - Tasleet (GB) - 6f maiden on good-to-firm at Chepstow, England - 2yo

July

01 - U S Navy Flag (USA) - 6f maiden on good-to-yielding at Curragh, Ireland, 2yo

02 - Gustav Klimt (IRE) - 7f maiden on good at Curragh, Ireland - 2yo

08 - Seahenge (USA) - 6f maiden on good at Naas, Ireland - 2yo

13 - James Garfield (IRE) - 6f maiden on good-to-firm at Doncaster, England - 2yo

14 - Hawkbill (USA) - 7f maiden on standard at Lingfield, England - 2yo

30 - Kessaar (IRE) - 6f novice on good-to-form at Windsor, England - 2yo

August

04 - Lancaster Bomber (USA) - 7f maiden on good at Leopardstown, Ireland - 2yo

14 - Order Of St George (IRE) - 1m maiden on soft at Leopardstown, Ireland - 2yo

18 - Roaring Lion (USA) - 1m novice on good-to-soft at Newmarket, England - 2yo

22 - Cloth Of Stars (IRE) - 1m newcomers on soft at Deauville, France - 2yo

27 - Saxon Warrior (JPN) - 1m maiden on yielding at Curragh, Ireland - 2yo

29 - Lightning Spear (GB) - 7f maiden on standard at Lingfield, England - 2yo

September

17 - Harry Angel (IRE) - 6f Group 2 on good-to-soft at Newbury, England - 2yo

21 - Massaat (IRE) - 7f maiden on good-to-soft at Leicester, England - 2yo

22 - Taareef (USA) - 1m conditions on soft at Bordeaux Le Bouscat, France - 2yo

30 - Seabhac (USA) - 8.5f Grade 3 on firm at Belmont Park, USA - 2yo

October

01 - Chemical Charge (IRE) - 1m maiden on good at Salisbury, England - 2yo

08 - Dylan Mouth (IRE) - 8.5f newcomers on soft at Capannelle, Italy - 2yo

19 - Cracksman (GB) - 1m maiden on good-to-soft at
Newmarket, England - 2yo

November

20 - Chanducoq (FR) - 10f conditions on good at Saint Cloud,
France - 2yo

NEW SIRES OF 2019
BY HIGHEST WIN LEVEL

Group 1 winners

Cloth Of Stars (IRE)

Cracksman (GB)

Dschingis Secret (GER)

Dylan Mouth (IRE)

Expert Eye (GB)

Guignol (GER)

Harbour Law (GB)

Harry Angel (IRE)

Havana Grey (GB)

Hawkbill (USA)

Jungle Cat (IRE)

Lancaster Bomber (USA)

Lightning Spear (GB)

Mekhtaal (GB)

Merchant Navy (AUS)

Order Of St George (IRE)

Poet's Word (IRE)

Recoletos (FR)

Roaring Lion (USA)

Saxon Warrior (JPN)

Sioux Nation (USA)

U S Navy Flag (USA)

Unfortunately (IRE)

Zoustar (AUS)

Group 2 winners

Doha Dream (FR)

Gustav Klimt (IRE)

James Garfield (IRE)

Kessaar (IRE)

Massaat (IRE)
Rajasinghe (IRE)
Seahenge (USA)
Sumbal (IRE)
Taareef (USA)
Tasleet (GB)

Group 3 winners
Chemical Charge (IRE)
Master Carpenter (IRE)
Seabhac (USA)
Smooth Daddy (USA)
Washington DC (IRE)

Listed race winners
Mr Owen (USA)

National Hunt blacktype winners
Tunis (POL) – NH-2

Non-blacktype winners
Chanducoq (FR)

NEW SIRES OF 2019
BY DISTANCE OF GROUP WINS

5f

Havana Grey (GB) - 2yo, 3yo
Sioux Nation (USA) - 2yo

5.5f

Unfortunately (IRE) - 2yo

6f

Harry Angel (IRE) - 2yo, 3yo, 4yo
James Garfield (IRE) - 2yo
Jungle Cat (IRE) - 6yo
Kessaar (IRE) - 2yo
Merchant Navy (AUS) - 3yo (inc 2 as NH 4yo)
Rajasinghe (IRE) - 2yo
Sioux Nation (USA) - 2yo, 3yo
Tasleet (GB) - 4yo
U S Navy Flag (USA) - 2yo, 3yo
Unfortunately (IRE) - 2yo, 3yo
Washington DC (IRE) - 4yo
Zoustar (AUS) - 3yo

7f

Expert Eye (GB) - 2yo, 3yo
Gustav Klimt (IRE) - 2yo
James Garfield (IRE) - 3yo
Jungle Cat (IRE) - 6yo
Massaat (IRE) - 4yo
Seahenge (USA) - 2yo
Tasleet (GB) - 3yo
U S Navy Flag (USA) - 2yo
Zoustar (AUS) - 2yo, 3yo

1m

Cloth Of Stars (IRE) - 2yo
Expert Eye (GB) - 3yo
Lightning Spear (GB) - 5yo, 6yo, 7yo
Recoletos (FR) - 4yo
Roaring Lion (USA) - 2yo, 3yo
Saxon Warrior (JPN) - 2yo, 3yo
Taareef (USA) - 3yo, 4yo

1m 0.5f

Seabhac (USA) - 2yo

1m1f

Master Carpenter (IRE) - 3yo
Mekhtaal (GB) - 4yo
Recoletos (FR) - 4yo
Smooth Daddy (USA) - 6yo
Taareef (USA) - 3yo

1m2f

Cloth Of Stars (IRE) - 3yo, 4yo
Cracksman (GB) - 3yo, 4yo
Dylan Mouth (IRE) - 4yo
Hawkbill (USA) - 3yo
Mekhtaal (GB) - 3yo
Poet's Word (IRE) - 5yo
Recoletos (FR) - 3yo
Roaring Lion (USA) - 3yo
Sumbal (IRE) - 3yo

1m2.5f

Cloth Of Stars (IRE) - 4yo
Lancaster Bomber (USA) - 4yo

Roaring Lion (USA) - 3yo

1m3f

Dylan Mouth (IRE) - 3yo, 4yo
Guignol (GER) - 4yo

1m4f

Chemical Charge (IRE) - 5yo
Cracksman (GB) - 3yo, 4yo
Dschingis Secret (GER) - 4yo, 5yo
Dylan Mouth (IRE) - 3yo, 4yo, 5yo
Guignol (GER) - 3yo, 4yo
Hawkbill (USA) - 4yo, 5yo
Poet's Word (IRE) - 4yo, 5yo

1m6f

Dschingis Secret (GER) - 3yo
Dylan Mouth (IRE) - 7yo
Order Of St George (IRE) - 3yo, 4yo, 5yo, 6yo

1m6.5f

Harbour Law (GB) - 3yo

1m7f

Doha Dream (FR) - 3yo

2m

Order Of St George (IRE) - 5yo

2m4f

Order Of St George (IRE) - 4yo

NEW SIRES OF 2019
BY AGE OF GROUP WINS

2yo

Cloth Of Stars (IRE)
Expert Eye (GB)
Gustav Klimt (IRE)
Harry Angel (IRE)
Havana Grey (GB)
James Garfield (IRE)
Kessaar (IRE)
Rajasinghe (IRE)
Roaring Lion (USA)
Saxon Warrior (JPN)
Seabhac (USA)
Seahenge (USA)
Sioux Nation (USA)
U S Navy Flag (USA)
Unfortunately (IRE)
Zoustar (AUS)

3yo

Cloth Of Stars (IRE)
Cracksman (GB)
Doha Dream (FR)
Dschingis Secret (GER)
Dylan Mouth (IRE)
Expert Eye (GB)
Guignol (GER)
Harbour Law (GB)
Harry Angel (IRE)
Havana Grey (GB)
Hawkbill (USA)
James Garfield (IRE)

Master Carpenter (IRE)
Mekhtaal (GB)
Merchant Navy (AUS) (inc. 2 as NH 4yo)
Order Of St George (IRE)
Recoletos (FR)
Roaring Lion (USA)
Saxon Warrior (JPN)
Sioux Nation (USA)
Sumbal (IRE)
Taareef (USA)
Tasleet (GB)
U S Navy Flag (USA)
Unfortunately (IRE)
Zoustar (AUS)

4yo
Cloth Of Stars (IRE)
Cracksman (GB)
Dschingis Secret (GER)
Dylan Mouth (IRE)
Guignol (GER)
Harry Angel (IRE)
Hawkbill (USA)
Lancaster Bomber (USA)
Massaat (IRE)
Mekhtaal (GB)
Order Of St George (IRE)
Poet's Word (IRE)
Recoletos (FR)
Taareef (USA)
Tasleet (GB)
Washington DC (IRE)

5yo

Chemical Charge (IRE)

Dschingis Secret (GER)

Dylan Mouth (IRE)

Hawkbill (USA)

Lightning Spear (GB)

Order Of St George (IRE)

Poet's Word (IRE)

6yo

Jungle Cat (IRE)

Lightning Spear (GB)

Order Of St George (IRE)

Smooth Daddy (USA)

7yo

Dylan Mouth (IRE)

Lightning Spear (GB)

NEW SIRES OF 2019
BY GOING DESCRIPTION FOR GROUP WINS

TURF

Firm

Harry Angel (IRE) - 3yo

Seabhac (USA) - 2yo

Taareef (USA) - 4yo

Good-to-firm

Dylan Mouth (IRE) - 7yo

Expert Eye (GB) - 3yo

Gustav Klimt (IRE) - 2yo

Harry Angel (IRE) - 3yo, 4yo

Havana Grey (GB) - 3yo

Lancaster Bomber (USA) - 4yo

Lightning Spear (GB) - 5yo

Merchant Navy (AUS) - 3yo (running as NH 4yo)

Poet's Word (IRE) - 5yo

Rajasinghe (IRE) - 2yo

Roaring Lion (USA) - 3yo

Sioux Nation (USA) - 2yo, 3yo

U S Navy Flag (USA) - 3yo

Washington DC (IRE) - 4yo

Good

Cloth Of Stars (IRE) - 2yo, 3yo, 4yo

Cracksman (GB) - 4yo

Doha Dream (FR) - 3yo

Dschingis Secret (GER) - 4yo, 5yo

Dylan Mouth (IRE) - 3yo, 4yo, 5yo

Expert Eye (GB) - 2yo, 3yo

Guignol (GER) - 4yo

Harbour Law (GB) - 3yo

Hawkbill (USA) - 4yo, 5yo

James Garfield (IRE) - 2yo

Jungle Cat (IRE) - 6yo

Lightning Spear (GB) - 6yo, 7yo

Mekhtaal (GB) - 3yo, 4yo

Merchant Navy (AUS) - 3yo

Order Of St George (IRE) - 3yo, 4yo

Poet's Word (IRE) - 5yo

Recoletos (FR) - 4yo

Saxon Warrior (JPN) - 3yo

Taareef (USA) - 3yo, 4yo

U S Navy Flag (USA) - 2yo

Unfortunately (IRE) - 2yo, 3yo

Zoustar (AUS) - 2yo, 3yo

Good-to-yielding

Havana Grey (GB) - 3yo

Good-to-soft

Cloth Of Stars (IRE) - 4yo

Cracksman (GB) - 3yo

Harry Angel (IRE) - 2yo

James Garfield (IRE) - 3yo

Master Carpenter (IRE) - 3yo

Recoletos (FR) - 4yo

Roaring Lion (USA) - 2yo

Saxon Warrior (JPN) - 2yo

Seahenge (USA) - 2yo

U S Navy Flag (USA) - 2yo

Unfortunately (IRE) - 2yo

Yielding

Order Of St George (IRE) - 5yo

Smooth Daddy (USA) - 6yo
U S Navy Flag (USA) - 2yo

Yielding-to-soft

Order Of St George (IRE) - 6yo

Soft

Cloth Of Stars (IRE) - 4yo
Cracksman (GB) - 3yo, 4yo
Dschingis Secret (GER) - 3yo, 4yo
Dylan Mouth (IRE) - 3yo
Guignol (GER) - 3yo, 4yo
Havana Grey (GB) - 2yo
Hawkbill (USA) - 3yo, 4yo
Kessaar (IRE) - 2yo
Massaat (IRE) - 4yo
Order Of St George (IRE) - 3yo, 4yo, 5yo
Poet's Word (IRE) - 4yo
Recoletos (FR) - 4yo
Roaring Lion (USA) - 3yo
Saxon Warrior (JPN) - 2yo
Taareef (USA) - 3yo, 4yo
Tasleet (GB) - 4yo

Very soft

Recoletos (FR) - 3yo
Sumbal (IRE) - 3yo

Heavy

Cloth Of Stars (IRE) - 3yo
Dschingis Secret (GER) - 4yo
Harry Angel (IRE) - 3yo

POLYTRACK
Standard
Tasleet (GB) - 3yo

Standard-to-slow
Chemical Charge (IRE) - 5yo
Kessaar (IRE) - 2yo

NEW SIRES OF 2019
BY FEE

Euros

€30,000 – Saxon Warrior (JPN)

€25,000 – U S Navy Flag (USA)

€20,000 – Merchant Navy (AUS)

€12,500 – Sioux Nation (USA)

€8,000 – Jungle Cat (IRE)
€8,000 – Kessaar (IRE)
€8,000 – Recoletos (FR)

€7,500 – Cloth Of Stars (IRE)
€7,500 – Gustav Klimt (IRE)

€7,000 – James Garfield (IRE)

€6,500 – Order Of St George (IRE)

€6,000 – Taareef (USA)

€5,000 – Mekhtaal (GB)
€5,000 – Seabhac (USA)
€5,000 – Seahenge (USA)
€5,000 – Smooth Daddy (USA)

€4,500 – Guignol (GER)

€4,000 – Chemical Charge (IRE)
€4,000 – Dschingis Secret (GER)

193

€3,000 – Mr Owen (USA)
€3,000 – Sumbal (IRE)
€3,000 – Tunis (POL)

€2,500 – Doha Dream (FR)

€1,400 – Chanducoq (FR)

Pounds

£40,000 – Roaring Lion (USA)

£25,000 – Cracksman (GB)
£25,000 – Zoustar (AUS)

£20,000 – Expert Eye (GB)
£20,000 – Harry Angel (IRE)

£8,500 – Lancaster Bomber (USA)
£8,500 – Lightning Spear (GB)

£8,000 – Havana Grey (GB)

£7,500 – Hawkbill (USA)
£7,500 – Unfortunately (IRE)

£7,000 – Poet's Word (IRE)

£6,000 – Tasleet (GB)
£6,000 – Washington DC (IRE)

£5,000 – Massaat (IRE)
£5,000 – Rajasinghe (IRE)

£4,000 – Harbour Law (GB)

£2,000 – Dylan Mouth (IRE)
£2,000 – Master Carpenter (IRE)

INDEX
(flat Group/Grade 1 winners and sires mentioned)

Printed in Poland
by Amazon Fulfillment
Poland Sp. z o.o., Wrocław